W9-CJN-178

FREEDOM BUILDERS

FREEDOM BUILDERS

GREAT TEACHERS
FROM SOCRATES TO JOHN DEWEY

by ROSE FRIEDMAN

Little, Brown and Company   Boston • Toronto

CARL A. RUDISILL LIBRARY
LENOIR RHYNE COLLEGE

COPYRIGHT © 1968 BY ROSE FRIEDMAN

ALL RIGHTS RESERVED. NO PART OF THIS BOOK MAY BE REPRO-
DUCED IN ANY FORM OR BY ANY ELECTRONIC OR MECHANICAL
MEANS INCLUDING INFORMATION STORAGE AND RETRIEVAL SYS-
TEMS WITHOUT PERMISSION IN WRITING FROM THE PUBLISHER,
EXCEPT BY A REVIEWER WHO MAY QUOTE BRIEF PASSAGES IN A
REVIEW.

LIBRARY OF CONGRESS CATALOG CARD NO. 68-15555

FIRST EDITION

370.922
F91f
90784
nov.1974

Published simultaneously in Canada
by Little, Brown & Company (Canada) Limited

PRINTED IN THE UNITED STATES OF AMERICA

To the Future Teachers of the World:
May they find that vital spark.

Education is the keystone
in the arch of freedom and progress.

JOHN F. KENNEDY

CONTENTS

FREEDOM BUILDERS

FLIGHT IN TIME

This book is concerned with some of the outstanding personalities who laid the groundwork for the teaching profession. In it you will meet teachers whose wisdom, vision, and dedication gradually established the foundation for a profession that in the United States alone now numbers almost two and three-quarters million teachers, supervisors, and administrators. They are largely responsible for the education of more than fifty-seven million young people from kindergarten through college.

Several of these teachers left little or no written record of their work, so we must piece together what their contemporaries wrote about them. More than half of those who did leave some account of their activities wrote in their native languages, so we must rely on translations to tell their stories, some of which contradict each other. The author lived so closely with these teachers while writing this book that occasionally she caught herself putting their thoughts into spoken words.

So timeless were the ideas and ideals of these teachers that they have helped to shape our thinking today. "Education," said the late President John F. Kennedy, "is the keystone in the arch of freedom and progress." If this is true, then the teachers have been and still are the chief builders of that arch — so long under construction and as yet so far from completion.

If you could "lift off" in a time-craft and orbit the ages to view these pioneers in action, you would find, as you whirled several times from the Present to the Past and back to the Present again, that the centuries are all of one piece, for what was Present yesterday is Past today, and what was Future yesterday is Present today. How far should you go to join them? For the first trip, a small slice of the ages, not quite twenty-five hundred years, would surely be enough; Athens, Greece, a good starting place.

For it was then and there that the citizens, having cast out their tyrants, recognized that each man has his own particular worth and the right to dignity. Then and there the freedoms of the mind were born: freedom to think, to reason, to question, to speak out, to disagree; freedom for each individual to reach for his own special brand of excellence. Here three teachers of that era will hold the mirror in which you can see that they had no easy time laying the foundation for "the arch of freedom and progress," for it had to be anchored firmly in the bedrock of enduring values.

The piers of the arch creep slowly upward, though upheavals have many times sent its blocks crumbling to the ground. But the firm base has always stood ready to be built upon again. Its keystone is still being shaped for its task of locking the whole arch together.

I

SOCRATES
MIRRORS MAN'S THINKING

In almost any section of Greece or its nearby islands
today, you are likely to come upon mounds of up-
turned earth, piles of rock, and yawning holes in the
ground. Here men and women — college students,
hobbyists, and seasoned archaeologists — are digging. They are looking for ancient relics which will
tell us about life in the distant past. They have the
proof, found by earlier searchers, that great cultures
existed many centuries before our civilization
evolved. But they go on hunting, hoping to fill a few
more blanks in our knowledge of prehistoric times
and seeking to make history of what has never
before been accepted as fact.

Other explorers — historians, philosophers, scholars — are probing for accurate evidence of what
men thought, what they were taught, and how

they learned in the long-past ages. For customs, they study the scenes that decorate the vases, jugs, sculpture, and architectural remains dug up by the archaeologists. For beliefs, they examine the ruins of famous temples, statues of gods and goddesses, and fragments of monuments found in one-time cities: cities that were buried one beneath the other as new civilizations grew up on those that had been devastated by war, invaders, and famine or deserted for other reasons. For activities, they ponder statues of athletes, burial stelae or gravestones, bits of household equipment, tools, and other artifacts that have been unearthed. For further information they analyze the myths and legends that were handed down by word of mouth, interpret decoded hieroglyphics, and pore over the wax tablets and papyrus manuscripts that served as the first books after the alphabet came into use.

Thus the searchers have brought many of antiquity's great personalities back to us, unfolding their stories, telling their secrets, showing their ambitions, even their thoughts. But always some "greats" remain shrouded in mystery, defying these history-hungry hunters.

One person has puzzled scholars for close to twenty-four centuries. Socrates of Athens, whose ideals and ideas have sifted through the ages down to us today, left no written records, yet many modern thinkers consider him the first great teacher. How do they know? Someone has said, "The greatness of a teacher depends on his ability to fashion great pupils." And Socrates was able to do exactly this. Had it not been for Plato and Xenophon, his two outstanding and most devoted disciples, the name of Socrates might have been lost to us, just as the names of other inspiring teachers in later centuries have been forgotten.

But even these two loyal pupils neglected to give us any account of their philosopher-teacher's boyhood. To rebuild the life of Socrates, we must put together the meager scraps of information available, then work backward in imagination to how he might have lived long before they knew him. Let us begin with five-year-old Socrates, in the year 464 B.C.

The small boy stands in the courtyard of his humble home, facing his "brave and burly" mother. His full lips are pouting, his eyes blurred with tears. His mother is his first teacher and she must instruct him in what is right and wrong. He sees from her expression that she believes him wrong.

"Why did you kick your brother, then run and hide like a coward?" she asks sternly.

"He's bigger than I am. He had my stone," Socrates blusters. "I made it smooth in the shop."

"Give it to me," his mother orders; and the child reluctantly holds out an oblong piece of yellowish marble, polished to a silken gloss.

"Did your brother take this from you?" his mother, Phaenarete, asks.

Young Socrates shakes his head. "I lost it near the cistern," he says, pointing to the water tank in the yard. "Patrocles found it."

"Did he know it was yours?" his mother asks.

Again the child shakes his head.

"Where did you get the stone before you polished it?"

"In father's shop," the boy answers.

"Then is it not as much your father's as yours?"

And before little Socrates can reply, his mother goes on: "And does it not belong as much to Cephalus who hired your father to buy the marble for his statuary?"

Phaenarete sees the puzzlement in her small son's eyes. Her heart softens and she hands back the polished stone. "Go now, Socrates," she says. "But next time remember that you must think before you act. You must be just in what you do."

For the rest of the day, the boy follows Sophroniscus, his father, in the shop and watches him chip a marble slab to shape the head of the newest statesman to be honored by the citizens of Athens. But the child's lips are pursed and his thoughts are far away.

That night in the corner of the bare, windowless room where the boys make their beds, Socrates suddenly surprises his brother. He holds out the smooth piece of marble. "Here, take it," he says. "You did not know it was mine. I kicked you and I ran away, because I could not fight you. I was not brave. I was not — not — just." He stumbles over the word, because he is not quite sure of its meaning.

No written document tells us of this scene in the childhood of Socrates, but it is typical enough of the home training of his time to make us believe that it

could have happened. And written records do give
the names of his parents and half-brother. His father was a freeman, and freemen, born and living in
Athens, were citizens. They were required to send
their sons to school from the age of six to the age of
fourteen — although there were no free public
schools in those days. The girls stayed home, learning household duties — weaving, sewing, in order
to make most of the things the family wore or used
in the home; they even learned to read and write, if
their mothers had enough education.

If we study the pictures on an ancient vase of
that period, we may see an eleven-year-old Socrates
standing barefoot and watching attentively as his
teacher demonstrates how to play the pipes. Behind
him stands another boy waiting patiently while his
teacher checks his wax tablet. A bearded peda-
gogue, the slave who accompanies a boy to school
and keeps an eye on him until his return home, sits
nearby watching his young charge.

The classroom where Socrates learned to read
and write, do his sums, and play the lyre may even
have been out-of-doors. He spent long afternoons in
the palaestra, the boys' gymnasium, drilling and
playing strenuous games, for the Greeks believed
that a strong body laid the foundation for a sound
mind.

We may visualize Socrates' disappointment
when his father took him out of school and apprenticed him to a sculptor. But we do not know how old
the boy was at the time, whether he had completed

only his elementary studies, or whether he had had
an opportunity for some higher education. On one
fact all agree, however. As Socrates grew into his
teens, he did not grow more handsome. A squat
young man, with head too large for his body, eyes
bulging above a flat nose, and thick lips frequently
pursed, he gave little thought to his appearance or
his dress. His mind was already too full of questions
and startling ideas to be bothered with less
important matters.

We can only guess how a wealthy young man
named Crito discovered this unkempt teen-ager.
Perhaps it was because they were about the same
age — in a democracy where people of all classes
mingled freely. Perhaps he had heard of the youth
and had watched him wandering barefoot through
the Agora, that rambling, hectically busy marketplace of Athens. Perhaps Crito stopped to listen one
day as the young thinker engaged a grain dealer in
conversation and pried out his reasons for charging
one customer more than another for the same
amount of grain. Crito must have chuckled as Socrates' sly questions drew out the merchant's fumbling
excuses. He must have been impressed as the man
gradually faced the fact that he had been wrong in
cheating the more trusting and letting the shrewd,
hard-bargaining customer have the advantage of
lower prices. Then Crito probably joined Socrates
and walked back to the shop with him to continue
the conversation on justice.

Again and again Crito talked with Socrates and

finally hired the youth to make him some statuary. Later, recognizing his amazing wisdom, he persuaded Socrates to study under a Sophist, a paid teacher of higher education. The Sophists tutored ambitious young men in rhetoric, debate, science, government, and other subjects considered necessary for those who might become the future statesmen of Athens.

Socrates' penetrating questions certainly gave his tutors a hard time, for they expected their students to take their words for granted. And this Socrates would not do. Some Sophists made fun of Greek beliefs, instead of teaching how customs and traditions must change to meet the changing times. Some scoffed at laws and insisted that material success was the only gain worthwhile. Others argued that ideals were nonsense made up by people who were too lazy to outwit the next fellow. Teachers of this sort gave the whole Sophist profession a poor reputation, so that the excellent, conscientious teachers among them were classified with the worst.

Socrates came away with little respect for most Sophists, because he saw through them. He saw how they could distort perfectly good ideas to make them serve their purposes. He saw how they taught their own opinions instead of getting at the basic truth underlying an idea. Socrates would have none of these teachings. His experience with these self-styled wise men inspired him to devote his later life to setting people straight in their thinking.

Socrates grew up in a period much like our

own. Athens, his city-state, with the help of her allies had won a second great war against formidable
Persia. Although the military might of her strongest
rival, Sparta, had made this possible, Athens was the
chief sea power in the world that encircled the Mediterranean Sea. After the defeat of Persia, the Spar-
tans returned to their agricultural life and aristocratic government and concentrated on developing
their whole community into a military state. But the
Athenians used their leisure to strengthen their democracy, increase their trade, and carry out their
conviction that every individual must develop to the
full extent of his capacities — and do this through
his own works. For protection, they organized their
allies into a peace-keeping confederation called the
Delian League.

Yet the rivalry of Sparta and other city-states
still plagued Athens. She knew that they watched
her growing trade with envy. She sensed that less
developed peoples could now see the advantages of
independence and power and might cause trouble.
So she gradually tightened her hold on the Delian
League, while Sparta gathered her satellites into a
Spartan Alliance.

About the time Socrates was born, a young
statesman in Athens was gaining fame as champion
of the people. Before long his name, Pericles, became a household word, for he introduced laws giving greater recognition and broader rights to every
free Athenian, rich or poor. He turned all his efforts
to making Athens "an education to Greece." He kept

her colonies in line, extended her power on the seas, beautified her in marble, and encouraged her writers, artists, and thinkers. His eloquent speeches taught the people the glory of their city. They inspired Socrates with unbounded patriotism and love for Athens.

More and more Socrates lingered in the Agora, where the assembly met, citizens voted, and festivities were held. More and more thoughtfully he listened to those who took advantage of the freedom of speech granted to Athenian men. On all sides he heard the endless discussion of politics and democratic liberties — although the privilege of citizenship was denied to women, foreigners, and the slaves that made up two-thirds of the population. He saw the majestic Parthenon, other temples, and dozens of statues of unrivaled perfection being erected on the Acropolis. He may even have stood on that rocky fortress beside the matchless sculptor Phidias and watched him chisel his own portrait and that of Pericles among the warriors he portrayed on the shield of the patron goddess, Athena — a deed which almost cost the artist his life. And if we agree with some scholars, Socrates gazed with satisfaction on his own bit of sculpture, a group of Graces adorning the Acropolis.

Athens in her Golden Age, at the height of her magnificent achievements, seemed an increasing threat to her rivals. Antagonism grew, and when the Athenians accepted a neutral city into the Delian League and gave her naval aid, Sparta retaliated.

In 431 B.C., Athens and Sparta, each with her allies, plunged into the Peloponnesian War which went on intermittently for twenty-seven years and finally crushed the power of Athens, the first great direct democracy.

Whatever his convictions about war, Socrates proved himself a remarkable soldier on the battlefield. His daring rescue of his friend and pupil Alcibiades during one of the first battles in the struggle made him a hero to his companions. His grim stand to the very end in the Battle of Delium is described by Xenophon and mentioned by Plato in his writings.

We may visualize Socrates after a gory fray, wiping the grime from his face and the blood from his sword, as he converses with soldiers gathered from the various cities allied with Athens. From them he learns more than the geography and history of their home territory. He draws out their inmost thoughts. Perhaps they praise his bold courage, but he counters with questions: What do you call courage? Is it to rush headlong into danger without thought for the consequences? Does it include the need to know when to be afraid? Does it include knowing when to withdraw and when to press on cautiously, in spite of being afraid? And the soldiers, challenged by his questions, return to their posts, still turning the discussion over in their minds.

Socrates took part in one Peloponnesian campaign or another for ten years. Then, after the brief truce of 421 B.C., he returned to Athens permanently and left the fighting to younger men. He recognized his mission now — to wage his battle in words. Now his constant occupation was listening to and engaging men in conversation — guiding them to examine their deepest convictions.

Time had done nothing to improve his looks. His coarse hair had thinned to bald spots, but his matted beard still bristled, his broad nostrils quivered, and his stocky body lunged forward as, by a simple question here and there, he goaded a young man into tearing his own arguments apart. To his listeners, Socrates was then like one of the gods in whom most Athenians still believed. Even the skeptics were held by his clear reasoning.

Wherever he went Socrates stimulated thinking in his companions. Today we consider him a "born teacher," but he never called himself a teacher. He did not claim, like the Sophists, to be a wise man. He admitted only that he was a "lover of wisdom," a philosopher whose purpose it was to tap the dormant wisdom of those who came to converse.

For this period in Socrates' life we have the first-hand records of Plato and Xenophon to help us picture that sturdy figure in his worn tunic, cloakless and barefoot, walking thoughtfully to the Agora. Here the hucksters shout their wares, foreign merchants exhibit their luxuries, shoppers haggle over prices, and men exchange news. A load of marble hauled in from Mount Pentelicus clatters toward the Acropolis, from whose height the ring of chisels echoes shrilly. But underneath the hubbub, the

voices of the "talk-loving" Athenians run on as
steadily as the surf against the shore of nearby Pi-
raeus.

As soon as Socrates comes into view, men leave
their various groups and start toward him. By the
time he has reached the colonnades edging the marketplace, his circle of pupils has gathered. As they
move to a stoa or shelter at one side of the Agora,
they begin to talk. Even before they settle into
order, the conversation grows into argument. Immediately Socrates turns moderator. What are they ar-
guing about so seriously? Last week it was virtue,
the week before it was friendship, and before that,
truth. Today it is justice, with Socrates directing the
debate by his questions. He never forces his opinion
on anyone. Most often he claims that he himself
does not know. "I came to learn, too," he insists.
"What is your opinion?"

Gravely, raptly, innocently, he listens until at
some half-thought-through comment he swings into
action. Question after question he hurls at the
speaker, until his wordy theories or illogical answers
collapse on their weak foundations.

Without tuition fees of any kind, Socrates taught
his disciples. He led men to find knowledge within
themselves. Many of his questions never brought
final answers, but they guided the students into
clearing their minds of false opinions and vague
ideas. They led them to examine their own beliefs
and arrive at conclusions based on genuine values.

"I am a gadfly," Socrates often said. "I sting you into thinking."

But the Agora was not the only meeting place for Socrates. Wherever people joined him or he joined others, he made that place a classroom. Let us follow him to the home of Polemarchus, where a group of young men have assembled. Socrates sits talking to his disciple's father. They have been discussing old age and the advantage that wealth gives to older people. Now Socrates asks the elderly man what he considers the greatest blessing his wealth has brought him.

The older man replies promptly that the most precious gift his riches have given him is peace of mind. Because of his wealth, he has had no need "to deceive or defraud others." So he hopes to leave this world a just and honest man, "owing neither offerings to the gods nor debts to human beings."

Here is the moment Socrates has been waiting for. By gentle questioning, he leads his host to admit that speaking truthfully and paying debts do not necessarily make a just man.

Then, when his father must leave the group for other obligations, Polemarchus becomes the target for cross-examination on one of his teacher's favorite topics — *justice*.

Back and forth fly question and answer until Polemarchus defines justice as "the art which gives good to friends and evil to enemies."

By cross-examination Socrates leads his disciple to tear down his own arguments, until the philoso-

pher's seemingly artless questions trap the young
man into facing some basic facts: *

SOCRATES: . . . *But let us consider this further point:
Is not he who can best strike a blow in a boxing match
or in any kind of fighting best able to ward off a blow?*
POLEMARCHUS: *Certainly.*
SOCRATES: *And he who is most skillful in preventing
or escaping from a disease is best able to create one?*
POLEMARCHUS: *True.*
SOCRATES: *And he is the best guard of a camp who
is best able to steal a march on the enemy?*
POLEMARCHUS: *Certainly.*
SOCRATES: *Then he who is a good keeper of anything
is also a good thief?*
POLEMARCHUS: *That, I suppose, is to be inferred.*
SOCRATES: *Then if a just man is good at keeping
money, he is also good at stealing it.*
POLEMARCHUS: *That is to be implied in the argument.*
SOCRATES: *Then, after all . . . the just man has
turned out to be a thief. . . . And so you . . . are
agreed that justice is an art of theft; to be practiced, for
the good of friends and for the harm of enemies. . . .
That was what you were saying?*
POLEMARCHUS: *No, certainly not, though I do not
know now what I did say; but I still stand by the latter
words.*

Now by a steady battery of down-to-earth questions, Socrates leads Polemarchus to see that to injure any man causes the injured to "be deteriorated

* *The Republic: Bk. I*

in that which is the proper virtue of man . . . justice." Here the philosopher is ready for a summing-up question.

SOCRATES: *Then to injure a friend or anyone else is not the act of a just man, but of the opposite who is unjust?*

POLEMARCHUS: *I think that what you say is quite true, Socrates.*

Does this end the discussion? By no means. The argument on justice continues through the ten books of Plato's *Republic*. Whether the questions are in the words of Socrates or of his pupil Plato, who put them into writing some years later, no one can say definitely. We may be certain, however, that this cross-examining technique of teaching was Socrates' own method of drawing out his students until they themselves learned to search their minds and hearts for accurate definitions and for genuine truth. The philosopher's precept *Know thyself* became their own.

Some of their ideas were contrary to the traditional beliefs of many Athenians. A few of the disciples used their newly found freedom-to-think to their own advantage. Alcibiades, a brilliant young man, turned traitor and went over to the Spartan side. Clever Critias headed the pro-Spartan Thirty Tyrants for their brief rule of terror in their native city, Athens, after her defeat. Gradually the wrath of some Athenians turned on the humble philosopher. "Socrates, the unbeliever, is responsible for this," they stormed. "He has put ignoble ideas into our young men's heads."

Certainly Socrates knew the danger in ignoring such criticism during this period of upheaval in Athens, but he went on leading his discussions as usual. Perhaps he expected to be taken to task much sooner. For Socrates was at least seventy years old when he was brought to trial for worshipping new gods and corrupting the youth of Athens. His accusers were an orator, an artisan, and a would-be poet. Five hundred citizens sat as judge and jury.

Socrates was his own defense lawyer and, in pleading his case, he scarcely seemed to take the accusation seriously. Rather, it was as if he were teaching a lesson to those who sat in judgment on him. He reminded the judges of the report that the Delphic Oracle, through the priestess for Apollo, had proclaimed him, Socrates, the wisest of men. This must have been a mistake, he was sure, for he had never considered himself wise, as did the Sophists.

To test the accuracy of this report, he had gone among all types of people, trying to find those who were genuinely wise. Instead, he discovered that the politicians thought they knew more than they really did, the poets were inspired but hardly knew the meanings of their own writings, and the artisans were good workmen but woefully ignorant of the values that really counted. Forcing men like these to face their ignorance, Socrates told the jury, had earned him many enemies, among them his accusers.

As for himself, the accused, his only wisdom came from recognizing how little he really knew.

As for corrupting anyone, why should he want to corrupt the very people among whom he had to live? And when Socrates urged those in the audience to come forward, if he had corrupted any of them or their sons, the eloquent silence was his most convincing witness. Socrates continued his testimony thoughtfully, sincerely, with dignity. After he had rested his case and the decision of the five hundred was counted, he was convicted by only sixty votes.

In those days of Athenian democracy, a citizen sentenced to death could choose an alternate penalty. He could agree to go into exile or pay a sizable fine instead. Again Socrates took the situation lightly. Actually, he told the assembled people, he should be rewarded by honorable recognition instead of punished for his services. He explained why the other penalties could not be acceptable to him. But above all, he said emphatically, he would not "hold his tongue." If they offered to let him go free, on the promise that he would stop guiding others in their search for wisdom, he would have to refuse, because he owed to God the duty of discoursing about virtue as "the greatest good of man . . ."

"Wherefore, O Judges," he concluded, "be of good cheer . . . and know of a certainty that no evil can happen to a good man, either in life or after death."

Many Athenians grieved over the unfair condemnation of Socrates and a few, among them Crito, arranged a safe escape for him. Socrates not only refused to take advantage of their well-meant plans but he led Crito to see that it was wrong for him to break the laws which he, as a citizen, had helped to create. Even unjust laws must not be broken, he emphasized. They must be changed by a vote of the people.

At sunset of the appointed day, surrounded by his weeping friends, Socrates cheerfully paid the penalty prescribed — death by poison. Even after he had drunk the fatal draught, his calmness shamed the others into restraining their sorrow.

Finally he said, "Crito, I owe a cock to Asclepius; will you remember to pay it?"

"The debt shall be paid," said Crito. "Is there anything else?"

Socrates was silent. Content that Crito would pay his debt to the "god of healing," he himself had cleared his debt to the laws of Athens — and left all future generations his debtors.

Most of us agree with Plato that Socrates chose to drink the cup of poison hemlock rather than surrender in his battle against ignorance, rather than abandon his philosophy that "the unexamined life is not worth living," that live or die, man must stand by his conviction of what is right. Others agree with Xenophon that Socrates accepted death so willingly because of his age, because he preferred to leave the world while his mind was keen and his body strong

— rather than live on another ten years and see himself grow dull and infirm.

How Socrates would have chuckled at those very disagreements! "I've given them something to think about, something to dig for, something to argue over. And if they never find out, let them admit that they do not know, as was my custom, then go out and seek again."

What do his reasons for scorning escape matter to us now? His wisdom, his ideals, his method of leading his pupils to discover for themselves the difference between the sham and the genuine, the wrong and the right, injustice and justice, cunning and wisdom, wishful thinking and truth, have survived the centuries. This is Socrates, master-builder of freedom and progress, as immortalized in the writings of his greatest pupil, Plato.

II

PLATO

CHAMPIONS IDEAS

Open a bulky newspaper any Sunday morning.
Check the items on schools, colleges, teachers, new
teaching methods, students' problems, scholarships.
You may find one or more in every section. Glance
over the new books in your local library or the cur-
rent magazines on newsstands. See how many fea-
ture such topics. Consult your radio and TV listings.
At least once a week you may tune in on a discussion
that includes students. Read the platforms of candi-
dates for political office. Education is often a major
issue.

Here, too, people are "digging" — not for relics
to prove the excellence of early civilizations, but for
alive young people who can perpetuate that which is
basically excellent and assure continued excellence
in the future. Today talent scouts, with the help of

teachers, are screening out superior students and urging them to compete for scholarships that will help them make the most of their talents. Teachers are also trying to stimulate the larger group of conscientious, average pupils to discover and measure up to their individual aptitudes.

The quest for excellence is everywhere.

Answer a summons from your guidance counselor during the spring quarter. You may learn that you have been selected for an honors class. Listen to the seniors in the school cafeteria, as they chatter through their hurried lunch. You may arrive at a fair count of those who have already been selected by the colleges of their choice. They have reached one standard of excellence. Others are worried or embarrassed because lesser known colleges have not yet given the nod to their letters of application.

"Before Sputnik, I could have had an athletic scholarship," growls one towering senior, whose averages make him barely eligible for the baseball team.

His parents think back to World War II, when the government waved its magic G. I. Bill that opened college doors to thousands of veterans at Uncle Sam's expense. "That's what made even mediocre colleges raise their standards," they rationalize. "They had to weed out the average students to make room for the top-notchers."

Philosophers have a longer range of vision. To them, ancient Athens set the standards. Here a great civilization developed because its leaders recognized that each individual had his own worth and the right to reach for a star. Here each citizen had the promise that, on his own ladder of achievement, he might climb as high as his neighbor.

The steady progress during the age of Pericles proved the wisdom of such equality. But the long war and the humiliating defeat by Sparta changed the attitude of many Athenians. They brought a growing distrust of a democracy that guaranteed equal rights to citizens who would not take equal responsibility for good government.

No wonder war-weary, confused Athenians flocked to Socrates, eager to argue questions that pulled them one way and another. Among these, one stood out in strong contrast to the homely, unkempt, elderly teacher. Handsome, strongly built, fastidiously dressed, well-educated, young Plato returned again and again to listen to the master — to nod, to argue, and to smile, even when his own inconsistencies were exploded by the philosopher's skillful questioning.

Plato's background did not train him for a humble part in life. On his mother's side, he could trace his ancestry back to Solon, the famous Athenian lawmaker. His father boasted descent from Codrus, the last king of Athens. Plato had been brought up to appreciate literature and the arts. He knew the poetry of Pindar, the tragedies of the great playwrights — Aeschylus, Sophocles, and Euripides — and the comedies of Aristophanes. He lived among the works of sculptors and architects like Phidias and Callicrates. He had been so well tutored that he wrote plays and poetry while still in his teens. He was so thoroughly drilled in athletics that he won prizes in famous games — some say even a wrestling match in the Olympics. In fact the name Plato, which has survived almost twenty-four centuries, was only a nickname — given to him because it meant *broad* — referring to his broad shoulders or broad forehead. Today no one thinks of him by his true name, Aristocles.

Born in 427 B.C. at the height of Athens' glory, Plato lived through her waning power and final surrender to Sparta. He chafed under the brutal rule of the Thirty Tyrants, two of whom were his own relatives. He was appalled by the revolution that restored the city to democracy, because he realized that the democracy rested on a crumbling foundation. Even so, he might have made politics his career had it not been for Socrates.

Plato was twenty years old when he first felt the magnetism of Socrates' reasoning. And for the next eight years the young man was the philosopher's most devoted disciple. As he listened and responded to Socrates' goading, he gained a new understanding of people in all walks of life. He began to see the difference between the amateur and the expert, the crafty and the sincere, the true patriot and the "summer soldier."

Gradually he came to realize that knowledge and understanding must go hand in hand with clear thinking. He grew convinced that the right kind of education for all citizens might correct the evils in the world through peaceful means instead of war. Plato had found a new kind of learning — one that came from searching his own mind. Inspired, he stored in his memory — and perhaps took down on wax tablets — many of the truths that Socrates guided his pupils to uncover.

Had Plato found his vocation? Not yet. From time to time he still weighed the possibilities of a career in statesmanship. Then, before he had fully made up his mind on a profession, he was shocked by the unfair accusation and conviction of Socrates. In his sorrow and bitterness, Plato blamed all Athens for the infamous execution. He may have realized that his outspoken loyalty to the old master had made some citizens eye him suspiciously also. At any rate, he left his native city, perhaps to forget, perhaps to find a better type of government elsewhere.

In Megara, Egypt, Cyrene, Sicily, and other places he visited, Plato was welcomed warmly by scholars. Here he saw other civilizations first-hand and could compare them with his city-state. He discussed, questioned, and pondered over the different customs, laws, governments, and rulers of foreign countries. But Plato never forgot that he was still a citizen of Athens. He interrupted these travels to fight for his city in the Corinthian War. Then he set out again.

In Italy he had met Dion, brother-in-law of Dionysius, the tyrant king of Syracuse, capital of Sicily. Apparently Dion found in Plato the same mental stimulation that Plato had found in Socrates, for he persuaded the traveler to accompany him to Syracuse and serve as his teacher. Before long he was so delighted with his progress under the Athenian master that he arranged a meeting between him and the tyrant ruler, hoping that the whole court might benefit from Plato's wisdom.

For Plato, this was an opportunity to speak out against the kind of government that gave despots every luxury and their subjects only oppression and misery. The court listened aghast, and Dionysius rose to his feet raging.

"Why have you come to Syracuse?" he bellowed at Plato.

"I came to seek a virtuous man," Plato replied with dignity.

"Well, by the gods, you have lost your labors," the tyrant shouted. "Your speech is that of a doddering graybeard."

Plato drew himself up to his full height. His eyes blazed as he retorted, "And yours that of a tyrant."

Fuming, Dionysius ordered his men to seize Plato. Panic filled the court. But Dion stepped forward and begged permission to speak. Impatiently, the tyrant heard him out, as Dion reminded him that Plato was renowned in Athens as one of their greatest scholars — that harming him would surely cause trouble between his city-state and Syracuse. "Let him go home and you will be rid of him," Dion urged.

Sullenly Dionysius yielded; and the next morning Plato boarded a galley homeward bound. He was pleased because his friend had so much influence with the despot. But his pleasure changed to alarm several days later, when the captain cast him ashore on the Island of Aegina, where he was promptly taken into custody. Now he realized the full extent of Dionysius' fury, and he waited for a death sentence. Here, too, his reputation came to his rescue. The officials of the island decided to sell him into slavery as a prisoner of war.

As he stood on the block facing a mob of curious bidders the next day, Plato saw more clearly than ever how little value the average man had in the eyes of tyrants. His conviction that only the right kind of government could do away with such injustice deepened. He barely heard the voices calling their bids. "All the governments I have seen are wrong," he murmured.

Suddenly a shout, "Thirty minae," caught his attention. He stared at the man who had offered this high price. Then, with an effort, he restrained all signs of relief. His rescuer was Anniceris, a philosopher whose friendship he had made in Cyrene. Within hours he was a free man. Within days he was back in his native land.

Plato was now forty years old. His understanding of mankind had increased and his knowledge of the world had broadened. His fresh mental picture of other governments and the sorry state of their peoples deepened his conviction that only properly educated citizens could produce a government dedicated to the welfare of every individual in the State. Perhaps he could be the one to give Athens the help she needed. But how?

The magnetic spirit of Socrates directed his course. Plato decided to share his experience and knowledge with those who wanted to learn. Like Socrates, he would question, encourage opinions on various topics, and debate all sides of each issue, until his students arrived at the basic truth themselves. Yes, he would carry on the work of his great teacher, but he would do it more methodically — not in chance meeting places, waiting for an opportunity to present an idea for argument. He would establish a school, so that the pupils would know exactly where to find the teacher. He would take only students who had an aptitude for learning. He would include specific subjects, like geometry and astronomy, to sharpen the mind and give the scholars facts to hold onto. But the kernel of their discourse would be the genuine values underlying ideas.

Almost immediately after his return to Athens, Plato visited a public park just outside the city. Once again he kicked off his sandals and walked barefoot in the velvety grass, drinking in the silvery beauty of the olive trees and the classic lines of the statues and fountains around him. As he entered the gymnasium, he felt again the bitterness of twelve years earlier, for here Socrates had often conversed with his disciples.

Plato had no time for sorrow now. In a flash he decided on a small estate close by for his school. The money collected by friends to pay his ransom had been refused by Anniceris; it would buy the property. He would call the school Academe, from the name of the park.

To the Academy came some of his former fellow students for discourse with Plato. Sons of the old master's pupils also came to learn under the new philosopher-teacher. Steadily, others eager for knowledge traveled from distant parts of the accessible world to hear Plato question theories and tear illogical opinions apart, until the valid truth stood clear.

Even his lectures on mathematics, astronomy, and other subjects stimulated the students to explore their own minds until they understood every detail in each topic. But conversation centered more often around *ideas* than facts.

Plato set up certain standards that guided his students in analyzing ideas such as truth, beauty, temperance, courage, virtue, and happiness, all of which Socrates had prodded his disciples into defining. He led them to consider his philosophy that ideas are more "real" than the concrete objects they may represent. He showed them that a table, a chair, an animal, a person eventually passes out of existence. But the ideas that represent such classes of objects still remain within the mind.

He guided his pupils to realize that nothing on earth is perfect. No matter how beautiful a picture may be, the artist sees that it could be still more beautiful. No matter how brave a man may be, he knows that he could be still more courageous. The better tutored a scholar is, the more he senses that he has only scratched the surface of knowledge. Plato showed further that these and other qualities do not mean exactly the same thing to any two persons. Thus, although man may never reach perfection, this goal is the ideal which leads him to ever greater achievement — and excellence.

Plato was not satisfied with interpreting ideas into spoken words only. He saw the value of writing down the development of these ideas. And since the definitions called forth by Socrates and his disciples had laid the foundations for his own teachings, Plato made his written records a permanent tribute to his beloved master. He wrote up each discussion in dialogue form with Socrates, as moderator, carrying on the quest for ideals to live by. In his best-known treatise, the *Republic*, ideal justice becomes the basis for an ideal government. Although he makes Socrates the chief character leading the dialogues, Plato cannot disguise the fact that here is his own theory of education — a plan that might give birth to his dream of a perfect society, a utopia.

Plato's ideal society would be governed by those who are gifted not only intellectually but in all desirable virtues. His talent search would begin with the children. He would have the authorities — obviously the wisest and most virtuous in the city-state — send out to the country all persons over ten years old. Thus there would be no one to taint the young with prejudice, greed, or unwholesome habits. The boys and girls remaining would live together as children of the State. Until the age of ten, they would have the usual Athenian training, at home until six or seven years old, then in school for more formal education, all centered around wholesome games, stories, and activities that develop high ideals and good health practices. Their school work would include music, reading and writing, physical education, and some form of mathematics at every stage.

From the age of ten to twenty years the emphasis would be on increasingly strenuous physical education and good mental and emotional habits. The last two years would be devoted largely to military training. During this time the teachers would be on the look-out for the natural aptitudes of each pupil. The gifted would be initiated into higher mathematics and astronomy. At the age of twenty, all would take rigid examinations. Those who failed to pass would end their schooling at this point and go into the various occupations of the workaday world — the trades, agriculture, quarrying, commerce — or any other vocation for which they were best adapted.

Those who passed the tests would be required to spend ten more years in study, concentrating on higher mathematics, astronomy, and the correlation of all their subjects. Then they would face another battery of tests. The individuals who failed to measure up in these examinations would be placed in high military positions. Their task would be to protect the State and its inhabitants. Those who passed, however, would continue their studies, applying themselves to philosophical reasoning for five more years. At the end of this time, they would have reached the next to the last rung on the ladder of excellence.

Since knowledge and wisdom have no far-reaching value until they are put into practice, these thirty-five-year-old scholars must then go out among the workers in their city for fifteen years. They must serve an apprenticeship in the various occupations of the State and "partake of their labors and honors, whether they are worth having or not." Only the few who came through this grueling practical-experience test would be worthy of governing their city-state. These men and women — for both sexes were to have equal educational opportunity — at the age of fifty would step over the topmost rung in their upward climb. They alone would meet the standards for "philosopher kings" or queens. From this first class of superior citizens would come the children to be educated for future philosopher-rulers.

Supported by the State, with no family ties or obligations (for the families of the two highest classes were to be communal), these true humanitarians would be ready now to concentrate all their energies on the welfare of the State. Personal ambition would play no part in their thoughts. In Plato's *Republic,* politics has attained an ideal meaning —

the science of selfless, dedicated management of public affairs for the supreme good of mankind.

Equal opportunity in education for citizens, regardless of sex or station in life, education that guides pupils to make the most of their individual aptitudes, education that recognizes that the State is only as good as its citizens — this was Plato's dream. That people working together in perfect harmony, because each is pursuing the course for which nature has best suited him, cannot fail to be happy — this was Plato's conviction.

Twenty years after he founded the Academy, Plato received another invitation to visit Syracuse. Tyrant Dionysius was dead and his irresponsible son, Dionysius II, had inherited the authority over the city. Dion, long-time friend of Plato, was worried about the ability of his nephew to rule wisely. He urged the philosopher to return, this time to teach young Dionysius.

To Plato, this was a wonderful opportunity to try out his theories of government. He might help the young ruler develop into a "philosopher king" who would, in turn, convert his city into an ideal republic. If he could succeed in Syracuse, he might change the world. Quickly he placed the Academy in the hands of a reliable substitute. Then he sailed for Syracuse to meet the thirty-year-old ruler.

At first the royal student went to work with a will. He even ordered the courtiers to study with him. His change of attitude was so evident that his advisers feared the end of his tyrannical power and their own high office. They spread rumors that Dion was plotting to seize the throne and that Plato was conspiring with him. Perhaps these rumors reached the young despot's ears. Perhaps the hard work and long hours of study necessary to master Plato's teachings were too much for his limited ability. At any rate, he soon lost his enthusiasm for philosophy.

Once again Plato became a virtual prisoner in Syracuse. His friend Dion could no longer intercede for him, since he had been banished from the city. Fortunately for the philosopher, Syracuse became involved in war; and young Dionysius reluctantly released his teacher.

Although Plato's experiment was a failure, his teaching in Syracuse seems to have taken some root, for five years later Dionysius himself sent for Plato. The philosopher was now sixty-five years old, yet he reluctantly accepted the invitation in the hope that he might thus help Dion gain permission to return to his homeland. Once more the unpredictable ruler lost interest in study, and he sidestepped all Plato's efforts to intercede for Dion. Recognizing defeat, Plato went back to Athens and continued his work in the Academy.

Plato spent forty years of his life lecturing, teaching, and writing his manuscripts. Students came from near and far to study under the great master. When they left, they spread his ideas in their own cities. Others replaced them in increasing numbers.

Some stayed on until they found their own philosophy of values. Certainly Plato must have achieved a good measure of the harmony he sought for all mankind, for he died peacefully at the age of eighty, while attending a gay wedding party.

Plato had his critics in his own day, as he has in ours. Yet in a world so small, with limited transportation, without printing presses to pour his books into the market, with no newspapers to advertise or comment on his writings, without radio and television to carry his voice and face to the people, his philosophy and ideals so captured the minds of the thoughtful that his Academy survived for nine hundred years and earned the distinction of being the first university in Europe. His works and influence have lived on for more than twenty-three centuries and will probably survive at least that many more.

Scholars are still putting his words to the test, no longer asking whether this is Socrates or Plato speaking. Philosophers ponder his theories. Students dissect his meanings. Educators point out his methods. Politicians weigh his recommendations. Clergymen assess his ideas on virtue. Many nod and say, "Remarkable! These are all-time truths." Some frown and denounce him as a fascist. "He proposes regimenting the whole State, with the intellectuals ruling, the soldiers guarding, and the masses of people doing the work." Others shake their heads and mutter, "Putting gifted children in the hands of the State! Removing parental influence. Communal families. A communist! How dangerous!"

Were we to put him on trial and judge him by our standards today, we would surely end up with a hung jury. New trials would continue down the ages, for none can deny the basic truth in Plato's utopian dream, his conviction that every individual must make the most of his God-given abilities, for his own happiness and for building a better society. None can deny Plato's dedication to teaching, as he led his students in their search for the fundamentals of excellence, the ideals to live by.

III

ARISTOTLE
ADVOCATES THE LIFE OF REASON

In 1961 the Western world awoke to the fact that a scholar and teacher may be the central figure in an almost priceless work of art. The treasure: a Rembrandt painting. The price: two million, three hundred thousand dollars. The title: *Aristotle Contemplating the Bust of Homer*.

Most viewers do not question this breathtaking price for an original painting by one of the world's great artists. But during the past three centuries, many have wondered why Rembrandt chose for his subject the philosopher who had lived nearly two thousand years before his own time and why he linked him with the blind bard who had chanted his epic tales at least five centuries before Aristotle's birth. Researchers, intent on finding the answer, learned that originally the characters in the masterpiece had not been named. In fact, the painting had had a number of titles, among them A *Philosopher* and A *Savant*. How then could they be sure that the subject was Aristotle?

Exploring further, they discovered that Rembrandt owned a bust of Aristotle and also one of Homer. Close scrutiny of the painting revealed another interesting fact. Engraved on the medal decorating the handsome chain worn by the subject in the picture is a likeness of Alexander. This was exciting proof, for that great conqueror had been tutored by Aristotle and had developed such respect for the heroic tales of Homer that he is reputed to have slept with a copy of them under his pillow. Thus the story unravels.

But why is Aristotle "contemplating," instead of *studying* or *looking at,* the bust of the poet? Here is the magic key that can unlock the thinking of the teacher-philosopher.

The painting in New York City's Metropolitan Museum of Art shows a carefully groomed, lavishly dressed man, probably at the height of his career. Clearly, Aristotle did not need to earn his daily bread. Early records tell us that his own income was adequate and that his marriage had added a considerable dowry. What made him devote his life to the routine grind of studying and teaching? Was it sheer love of the work itself or some other goal that spurred him ever onward? Only a few of this amazing scholar's many manuscripts remain to show the devotion with which he followed in the footsteps of his famous teacher, Plato. These show us, too, the integrity with which he insisted on his own practical ideas when he disagreed with the idealistic theories of that great thinker.

Aristotle, the last of the noted Greek-philosopher trio, was born in 384 B.C. in Stageira, a town in northeastern Greece, far enough away from Athens to be considered barbaric by its cultured citizens. His father was a well-known physician in the court of Amyntas II, king of Macedonia. Curious and interested in everything about him, young Aristotle learned much about science from his environment. His father belonged to an ancient medical sect that expected its members to pass on their knowledge of medicine to their sons, in those days when no textbooks existed. So it is quite likely that the boy had planned to make a career of medicine, until the death of his parents left him in the care of a guardian.

How the youth came to make the long journey to Athens and to Plato's Academy there, we can only guess. There is even some question as to when he entered the Academy, but most authorities agree that he was in his late teens. If so, he studied, carried on research, and taught under Plato for twenty years, until the old philosopher's death. But during this time Aristotle proved to be no passive pupil. Many a fiery argument blazed between teacher and pupil. Aristotle had been deeply impressed by Plato's precept that knowledge must come from within the learner and that wisdom grows from a combination of experience and self-examination. So until he tore every idea apart, analyzed each thoroughly, then gave it a practical evaluation, the scholar refused to accept his teacher's theories. And Plato, recognizing the young man as his most promising student, gave him free reign, often against his own convictions.

Even before Plato died, the Athenians were again in violent disagreement over how to meet a new foreign aggressor. King Philip II was now ruler of Macedonia. Visualizing the power in a united Greece, he tried to persuade the separate city-states that, combined with Macedonia, they could conquer Persia and free the Greek colonies in Asia Minor. Some in Athens favored Philip's plan. Others, siding with the vehement orator Demosthenes, stood firmly against giving up their independence, especially to a "barbarian" king. So Philip set out on his own to conquer one city after another.

Fired by patriotism, the Athenians grew suspicious of all who sympathized with Macedonia, even their famous scholars in the Academy. So Aristotle found this the right time to accept an invitation from a former fellow-student to make his home in Asia Minor. He went first to Assos where Hermeias, his host, held a position of considerable power. Here he taught in a philosophical school for three years; and during this time he wooed and married the niece of Hermeias. His reputation as a scholar and teacher spread steadily.

But when Hermeias became involved in political intrigue, Aristotle grew uneasy; and when the situation became dangerous, he and his wife traveled on to Lesbos where he had other friends. This island was just the place to renew Aristotle's enthusiasm for nature study. He settled down to collect and organize a large assortment of biological specimens. Content in this scientific project, he might have stayed on indefinitely, but a sudden summons from King Philip changed the pattern of his life.

Already the Macedonian ruler's powerful armies and successful use of the phalanx battle formation had made him a famous conqueror. Now he wanted to leave a well-educated heir on the throne when he himself was gone. So he looked around for the best available tutor for his son Alexander. Indeed, the tutor had to be good, for even as a child Alexander was an unruly, self-willed boy who showed little respect for authority. The king's victories brought no congratulations from his son — only the surly complaint, "He is leaving me no worlds to conquer."

Very likely Philip, who was about Aristotle's age, had known him when his father was court physician. One story tells that King Amyntas spent his summers hunting in Stageira with the physician, and sometimes both young Aristotle and Philip were in the hunting party. Whatever the truth, Aristotle's scholarship had come to the attention of the king, who invited him to educate his thirteen-year-old son.

If Aristotle kept any diary of his experiences while trying to tame the future military genius, it is among the many manuscripts that have disappeared. How much Alexander learned under the philosopher's guidance is still a question for debate. Some historians assure us that during his conquests Alexander spared Greek culture, because he had learned to appreciate it. Some say that he spared or crushed cities, according to whatever whim swayed him at the time. Other scholars trace the trail of Greek culture that followed the conqueror to the far corners of his empire as proof of Aristotle's influence.

We cannot even be sure how long Aristotle worked with the young prince. Certainly no more than three or four years, for when Alexander was barely sixteen years old, the king made him his regent, and Aristotle's tutoring duties ended. He returned to his native Stageira and found it devastated by war. Immediately he appealed to the king to help his people, and King Philip gave Aristotle the task of supervising the rebuilding of the city and the return of its inhabitants.

During the next three years Greece was conquered, King Philip was murdered, and Alexander began his own whirlwind campaigns. Aristotle returned to Athens. Already he was famous in his own right, and since his adopted city seemed to have accepted Macedonian control, he felt doubly at home. The fascination of study drew him toward teaching, but with Plato gone, the Academy no longer interested him. A new school was the solution.

Since only Athenian citizens had the privilege of owning property in Athens, Aristotle rented some buildings and grounds on the outskirts of the city. He called his school the Lyceum, from the name of the temple, Apollo Lyceus, which it adjoined. But Aristotle did more of his teaching pacing the covered walks among the gardens than indoors. In fact, this habit gave his students the name of peripatetic scholars, from the Greek word *peripatetikos,* meaning "walking about."

Let us stroll along with the flashily dressed master, now in his early fifties, as he walks slowly toward his zoological garden. Listen to him talking gravely with the group of men, young and old, who keep step with him. No one notices his slight lisp. No one is distracted by the heavy gold rings and other finery that adorn him. It is plain that Aristotle has trained his disciples to concentrate on the topic under discussion. We translate his words into modern conversation. "Seeing is believing. Look at a fish, at a snake, at a bird, at a goat, at a human being. How are they alike? How are they different? What is their function in life? How do they fulfill it? Man alone has the power to reason out these and other truths. You are here for that purpose. Now get busy and find the evidence."

The men move on, conversing thoughtfully. They fall silent as they pause to check an experiment which they are performing. Twenty incubated eggs are giving "concrete evidence." Beginning with the second day after incubation, the master has broken open one egg daily and directed his students to observe the contents carefully. Day by day they have watched the embryo with its one little throbbing red spot. Now, on the tenth day, he opens the ninth egg. A murmur runs through the group. The chick has formed. Its parts are clearly visible.

"This much Alcmaeon discovered more than two centuries ago. You must carry on further. What of the human embryo?" Aristotle asks. "How must it be similar? How may it be different? Record your deductions. Compare and classify them."

Here conjecture begins, for the ancient Greeks would have considered dissecting the human body a sacrilege. Instead, they must observe, compare, draw conclusions, test, and retest.

In the Lyceum, the teacher and his students gathered a mass of hit-or-miss information of the past and held it up for rigid inspection. Natural science had always fascinated Aristotle. Under his direction, the scholars helped analyze, classify, and arrange his numerous specimens on the basis of their similarities and differences. Several historians credit Alexander with making possible his tutor's extensive experiments in biology. One tells that the young king and conqueror ordered his own "hunters, fishermen, and gamekeepers" to keep on the lookout for unusual materials for Aristotle's experiments. Another states that Alexander contributed the equivalent of several million dollars to pay a thousand men for collecting specimens throughout the known world for the work in the Lyceum. However he was financed, Aristotle's amazing achievements in this field led many to honor him as the "Father of

Biology." Even those who remind us that earlier scientists conducted similar experiments agree that Aristotle was the first to develop practical scientific methods of experiment and study. What is more, his students had the benefit of learning by doing.

It is true that Aristotle's conclusions were more often based on observation than on actual experiment, but the scientist within him refused to accept mere theories. We can almost hear him saying, "Question, define, dig out the why's of life — but be realistic. Take your hypothesis; put it to the test of closest observation and experiment. Check what you see against what others would have you believe. Then draw your conclusions. But do not be random. Keep everything classified and catalogued, as a guide for new observations."

Today's scholars point out countless mistakes in Aristotle's scientific conclusions, but too often they neglect to mention the meager equipment with which he worked. Let the critics picture one of our present-day experts mysteriously transported to that scientist's makeshift laboratory in the Lyceum. Without microscopes, telescopes, spectroscopes, thermometers, barometers, accurate scales, and a score of other instruments that he considers essential to his experiments, how much would he accomplish? And how he would miss his photographic equipment!

Aristotle, like Plato, pondered over politics, but he was critical of his old master's ideal republic. He made practical studies of one hundred fifty constitutions of Greek cities. He grouped them into types of government, analyzed each category, and showed the advantages and pitfalls in each — monarchies, aristocracies, oligarchies, democracies. He had no use for a democracy that yields to the unthinking mob. Like Plato, he thought even less of tyrannical governments. But he did not believe that Plato's dream government could work. He concluded that any government in the wrong hands can be destructive, and suggested a middle course — a combined aristocracy and democracy, with a strong middle-class to hold the demogogues in check. But how could this be made to work any better than the others? By education. By training both citizens and future administrators in integrity and concern for public welfare.

"Man," says Aristotle, "is naturally a social being." He is first a member of a family. But the family needs other families, so they gather in a village. The village needs other villages — which unite into a state. From these observations, Aristotle concludes that "man is also a political animal." He joins with others for his own and the common good. In this way, each has an opportunity to use his inborn capacities more fully. Yet no two people have exactly the same abilities. Even those whose interests seem identical may have widely different ambitions.

We can apply Aristotle's observations to modern life. Some businessmen, for example, exert all their energies to amass a fortune. Why? One wants money to give him the luxuries he yearns for. Another wants money to provide comforts for his old age. A father wants money so that his family may have an easier life than he had when he was young. A philanthropist delights in his millions because he can use the money to help the needy, finance scientific expeditions, or set up scholarships for young people.

Others aim for a career in statesmanship. Why? One is ambitious for power, another for personal prestige, a third believes that he can use this power to make a better world.

There are those who have special aptitudes for skilled labor. What are their goals? One is content to earn just enough to keep himself and his family comfortably clothed and fed. A second gets personal satisfaction from working with his hands. A third hopes that he can improve the machines, so that they can make better products.

Astronauts risk life and health to venture into outer space. Why? One is spurred on by his sense of duty. A second satisfies his pioneering spirit by orbiting the earth. A third craves glory, a fourth scientific information. A fifth believes that exploring the great unknown and establishing bases on the moon may be the best preventative against further wars.

But these are widely different goals. Is there then no single goal that all people, whatever their interests, abilities, or stations in life, have striven for through the ages? Yes, says Aristotle. That goal is *happiness*. Each person hopes that achieving his other ambitions will bring him happiness. Happiness cannot make money, bring renown, make scientific discoveries, or accomplish any other practical aims of mankind, yet it always shines in the distance ahead — the final goal.

Aristotle's definition of happiness is not the feeling of momentary elation brought on by some great success or yearned-for accomplishment. To Aristotle, happiness is a permanent condition, in which one "lives according to the highest that is in him, and that is his power of thought." *This* must be his objective. "Man is the only animal capable of reason," Aristotle writes. Because of his ability to reason, he can learn to think so clearly that he can recognize the true virtues and live up to them. It is his ability to reason that lifts him to the "human" kingdom and closer to the divine kingdom. Those who reach a state where they can go through life not only contemplating genuine values but acting upon them have approached Aristotle's standard of happiness. "Perfect happiness, therefore, is activity of thought . . . that is used for the highest purposes." Man must be educated to direct his gift of reason to this end.

How does this philosophy stand the test of present-day reasoning? Our world has grown through vastly extended settlement and increased population. It has shrunk immeasurably through improved means of transportation and communication. Yet civilized mankind agrees more and more that the native abilities of each individual must be developed as fully as possible by education. They agree that such education benefits not only the individuals themselves but the society in which they live. And they pride themselves on the thought that this is a modern philosophy — unless they look back.

More than twenty-three hundred years ago, Aristotle had the same idea. He made recommendations on education so far-reaching that, translated into modern language and applied to present-day conditions, they appear in thousands of our textbooks on teaching and educational psychology. Aristotle combined Socrates' credo that man must examine his own thinking and identify the basic values in life with Plato's vision of a society in which each individual has learned to use his fully developed capacities for the common good. He believed, as we do today, that "education is a life-time process" and that "excellence comes from the habit of making wise choices." He was firmly convinced that we must educate for peace and thus build for freedom and progress.

Broader and broader grew the studies of the master and his students. Deeper and deeper he probed in his teachings. On and on went the analyzing, classifying, and cataloguing. No wonder Aristotle collected a library that some authorities consider the first to be worthy of that name. His own manuscripts probably numbered between four hundred and a thousand. To what heights he might have taken his students we cannot know, for suddenly, in 323 B.C., word came that Alexander was dead.

To the Athenians, it seemed incredible that the young king who had pushed his conquests as far as India should have yielded to a greater conqueror — Death. Assured that the news was accurate, the people let loose their long-hidden hostility against Macedonian sympathizers. Away with them! Against Aristotle, who had remained openly loyal to his one-time pupil, the Athenians vented particular fury. They charged him with impiety.

Aristotle, like Socrates, had deep respect for the law; but he had no regard for lawlessness. He refused to let the Athenians "sin twice against philosophy." So he tied up the loose ends in the Lyceum, put a fellow-teacher in charge, and set out for Chalcis, his mother's homeland. He became ill and died there one year later, at the age of sixty-two. But his spirit, catching up with those of the two older master builders, has traveled with them through the ages, bidding us to take note of the values he reached for.

Surely both Socrates and Plato would accept the ideal of happiness that Aristotle insists is man's chief aim in life — the exercise of his power of thought until he is seeing clearly the ultimate good for all mankind. Then at last he stands on the topmost rung of his ladder of excellence. For those who have reached this permanently happy state of *contemplation* this is no passive life. These are the true philosophers — the devoted teachers and all those who guide the thinking of others toward eternal truth, through their precious gift of reason.

Gaze again at the magnificent Rembrandt painting — at the philosopher of encyclopedic knowledge deep in contemplation over "the father of all
poetry." Need we wonder whence came its title, *Aristotle Contemplating the Bust of Homer?*

IV

THREE ROYAL PROTÉGÉS
EDUCATE FOR FREEDOM AND PROGRESS

Each year thousands of visitors in Washington, D. C., tour the National Archives Building. Many entering from the Constitution Avenue side casually read an inscription: "The heritage of the past is the seed that brings forth the harvest of the future," without giving thought to the meaning of the words. But others pause to study the statue of the woman and the child symbolizing Heritage and to analyze the quotation beneath it. These thoughtful persons may well share educator Harold Taylor's conviction: "It is through the teacher that each generation comes to terms with its heritage, produces new knowledge, and learns to deal with change."

When President Kennedy stated that "a free nation can rise no higher than the standard of excellence set in its schools and colleges," he was echoing

Thomas Jefferson's warning: "If a nation expects to be ignorant and free . . . it expects what never was and never will be." Both Presidents saw education as the keystone to the Great Society.

But forward-looking heads of nations or peoples have not been confined to the North American continent, nor to the recent centuries. All down the ages some few stand out for having recognized the vital role of education in building a better world; and some of those who strode most boldly forward had beside them teachers who directed their steps toward this goal.

After Greece had been humbled and her cities disintegrated by conquest and petty jealousies, its schoolmasters found various ways of passing on the wisdom of the sages. Some continued in Athens and other cities in Greece. Some had already settled down to teaching in parts of Alexander's empire. Others migrated to Rome and set up schools in private homes, in shops along the Forum — the Roman marketplace — and even on the street. Thus Greek teachers influenced the development of Roman schools.

During the years of embattled Greece, Rome was busy building her Republic. With her harsh *Twelve Tables of Laws*, she had insured discipline and cooperation. With practical foresight, during the next two centuries she conquered or drew the neighboring settlements and Greek cities in Italy into an alliance for mutual protection against invaders. After more than one hundred years of intermittent warfare, she finally conquered African Carthage. Then Rome gradually extended her domain until it encompassed the Mediterranean.

All this time Greek culture had been seeping into Roman life. As soon as Greece became a part of the Empire, learned Greeks, enslaved as booty of war, were prized as tutors. Roman grammar schools for instruction beyond the primary level had sprung up even earlier; and soon the aristocracy began to see that a broader education would give them greater prestige as well as valuable knowledge. Wealthy young men increasingly traveled to Athens for advanced education. When schools for higher learning were gradually established in Rome, they specialized in oratory, which was considered essential for a career in statesmanship. As in Athens, the value and success of a school depended upon the knowledge, sincerity, and purpose of the teacher.

In Rome we find the man who is noted as the first public school teacher.

Quintilian

It is the year A.D. 70, late on a summer afternoon. Suddenly a group of boys rush from a schoolroom into a narrow street adjoining the Forum. A number of older students walk apart from the others, talking seriously. They have just completed their grammar school education. Now most of them are sixteen years old and must make up their minds on future careers. Some have decided that they need no further formal instruction but several plan to go on to schools of rhetoric. One is especially lucky, for he has been accepted by what amounts to an Ivy League school of his day. He will study under the great Quintilian, a rhetor with new ideas of how pupils should be taught — a master who believes that his students should work hard but should also be respected.

Marcus Fabius Quintilianus, more commonly known as Quintilian, was born in Spain, about A.D. 35. His father had been a successful teacher of public speaking in Rome, which may have been his reason for having Quintilian instructed in that city. A thorough, all-round education by capable teachers prepared the young man for a position in public life; and for a time he served as an advocate, pleading cases in court. But his fame grew from his success as a rhetor, a teacher of oratory. His school became so popular that it gained the attention of Emperor Vespasian, who ordered Quintilian paid out of the royal treasury, thus making him the first teacher with a salary financed by the state.

Success, recognition, and happiness seemed to come naturally to the scholarly rhetor. Quite late in life he married a girl much younger than himself, and in the next few years he became the father of two sons. Then misfortune struck. His wife died when she was only nineteen years old. But her legacy to him, the two small boys, eased his grief until the younger son, barely five years old, fell ill and died — "robbing me, as it were, of one of my two eyes," Quintilian wrote. The other child, little Quintilian, developed into the kind of lad every parent yearns for. His splendid character, his talent for learning, his perceptiveness and understanding inspired his father to try to make teachers realize the need for bringing out the talents of their pupils. Then tragedy struck again. Just when young Quintilian gave promise of "rising to all high offices of the state and rivaling the eloquence of his grandsire," as his father had prophesied, he suffered a long illness from which he did not recover.

Quintilian had begun to write his *Institutio Oratoria,* partly as a guide for parents, students, and teachers. His greatest hope, however, was that his son might inherit it. Now, having outlived the three dearest to him, Quintilian continued to write, spurred on by his deepening concern for the sons of all mankind. His surprisingly modern treatise, consisting of twelve sections which he called "books," became a legacy to posterity. The text presents an accurate picture of the best teaching in the schools of Rome at that time and also some sound criticism of the poor educational practices. But more important is his modern philosophy of how teaching should be conducted and students should be instructed.

Let us accompany the fortunate young grammar school graduate the day he begins his higher education. He seats himself in a cheerful, comfortable classroom, ready to listen, take notes, or answer questions. He relaxes during Quintilian's cordial, well-chosen words of greeting. He leans forward eagerly as the handsome, dignified rhetor begins the class period.

"The material of rhetoric," Quintilian explains, "is composed of everything that comes before the orator for treatment." He goes on to state that the pinnacle of education is oratory.

Nonsense! we think, until he adds that rhetoric must include a thorough knowledge of literature, accurate information on any subject concerning which an orator might be expected to speak, and the ability to select from an extensive vocabulary the words precisely appropriate to his subject. He must have an understanding of people and a sense of how words can open up ideas for them. But above all, Quintilian emphasizes, the orator must be a *good* man — a man who has "excellence of character, loftiness of soul . . . and will speak out clearly what he knows."

The faces of the students brighten. They begin to understand why Quintilian believes oratory is the ultimate goal in education.

Since they are beginners, he tells his class, he will give them an easy assignment — one similar to those given in grammar school. They are to compare the works of two authors with whom they are already familiar. But the requirements will be far more exacting than those in grammar school. "The art of rhetoric," he points out, "is the science of speaking well, and not necessarily the power of persuasion."

Quintilian's voice deepens, as he enumerates some important points to his attentive class. They are to "instruct" their audience by stating their cases accurately, clearly, honestly. They must praise what is good and criticize frankly what is inferior. They must move their hearers by their sincerity and by their understanding of their theses. The rhetor's eyes shine and his voice swells as he says dramatically, "Delight your audience by the quality of your ideas, by beginning where you ought and ending where you ought, by speaking in clear, well-modulated, flexible tones, and avoiding affectations or flowery words.

"Keep in mind that your talk will tell us how well you read and think, in addition to what further instruction you need. But" — Quintilian pauses for a moment, then spaces his words forcefully as he concludes: "Think your speech through before you organize it. Remember that next to writing, premeditation is of greatest use."

Does this have a familiar ring? Is it much different from the instructions an English teacher might give to a class today? Yet these directions are almost nineteen hundred years old.

Quintilian's interest did not begin and end with rhetoric. Parents and teachers, he wrote, should set good examples for children. The young can be stimulated to learn through play long before school age, if they are given interesting activities that lead rather than force them to learn. Public schooling is preferable to private tutoring, because it gives children the experience of associating with others.

Quintilian emphasizes that inferior teachers have no place in any period of a child's education. A teacher must be a man of sense. He should be friendly but not to the point of familiarity. He must watch for the natural aptitudes of his pupils and key his lessons accordingly. He should keep his teaching so interesting that he does not need to flog children. And he should "every day say something worthwhile that the pupils may carry away with them."

Where did Quintilian get these ideas? From Plato? From Aristotle? From his own experience in teaching? Were they fads and frills? Some Romans considered them so. From time to time the authorities had frowned on schools of rhetoric as merely "a waste of time" and even ordered them closed. But Quintilian gave them new status. Emperor Vespasian appointed him to one of the first public professorships in the city of Rome. Emperor Domitian entrusted the education of his two nephews to the famous rhetor. He rose to the rank of consul.

And although we are so vague about the date of his death that we must place it somewhere between A.D. 95 and 110, we know that schools continued to flourish in Rome, some under mediocre teachers, some under superior teachers, long after Quintilian. But unless we dig into musty volumes, we hear no mention of them. Education was on the downward path.

Rome's phenomenal rise had been at the expense of her early Republic. Her territorial gains, her amazing achievements in engineering, her vast system of roads, her huge building projects, her spectacular entertainments, her increasing luxuries, had blinded the aristocrats to the fact that twelve times *Twelve Tables of Laws* cannot build cooperation in oppressed peoples. Education, which had served to "Romanize" the whole empire, had come to be for the wealthy, for those who already had prestige. Why should the masses be interested? They were far more interested in the growing new religion, Christianity, that promised a better life in the next world, than their miserable existence on earth. When increasing hordes of barbarians invaded Rome, the common people had few reasons for resisting them. New conquerors could make their lot no worse. They might even improve it. True, they were wiping out culture and education. But the new religion taught that these were the godless ideas of pagans. Better that they should go.

But Quintilian's ideas on education had not only awakened the interest of rulers, they had directed the thinking of other teachers. As the sunset of learning seemed to be fading into darkness, these teachers, most of them nameless and fameless today, fanned the flickering light of knowledge and kept a glimmer for those who would later quicken it to radiance.

Alcuin

In the dimming light, we see reflected the straggling march of teachers who, for the next ten centuries, sprinkle seeds of learning along the way. Occasionally one comes who scatters seeds that start new growth. Here comes Charlemagne, the great ruler of the Frankish empire. He strides to keep pace with a tall, frail scholar who dares to step ahead, ever turning, as if to urge that majestic figure to press on.

Full of eagerness to know, Charlemagne cannot be content with his grandfather's Palace School which trained the young in courtly etiquette. He has known about the wondrous culture of Greece and Rome and has pondered long over how to bring it to his own people. The clergy warn against all worldly show and the king himself frowns on wanton pleasure-seekers. But he will not shut his eyes to the woeful ignorance of his populace.

It is the year 781, and the great Charles, with part of his family and an army escort, is on his way back to the royal palace in Aachen, his Germanic capital, after nearly a year in Rome. He thinks over his trip with satisfaction. En route, he had made his presence felt among his subjects and settled many problems. He had seen his two sons baptized by the Pope and crowned for their future roles as rulers. The Pope is finally acknowledging Rome to be part of the Frankish Empire. Still the king is restless.

On this trip he has had more time to linger among the marvels of Italian cities and listen to the talk of learned men. Now, as he rests in Parma, Italy, his mind is on a Saxon deacon with whom he conversed the day before. What a wise and informed man, this Alcuin! The king is aflame with a new ambition. Finally, he throws back his cloak and puts his thoughts into words.

"The strength of a kingdom lies in the wisdom of its people more than in the outward show of princely manners," he says to his queen, Hildegard. "We must educate them as well as our own children."

Before the queen has a chance to comment, Charlemagne goes on, "And to do so, we must secure the best of teachers."

"But you are taking Paul the Deacon back from Italy with you, and you already have Peter of Pisa and his assistants," the queen reminds her husband.

"They are good, but we need someone even better — someone to speed the zest for learning beyond the palace walls," the king insists. "Only thus can we unite all our subjects. Knowledge and culture will help them understand our purposes and give them pride in their country."

He halts his restless pacing and stands gazing into space. "Alcuin would be the man. This Alcuin of the Cathedral School of York. The Saxon I spoke of yesterday. The one who visited our court some years ago. He is yet in Parma, but soon to return to Britain, now that his mission is ended."

It took persuasion by Charlemagne, careful consideration by Alcuin, and permission from the archbishop in York before the scholarly deacon decided to accept the invitation. Only after he pictured the good he could do in the barbarian country and promised to return to the Cathedral School was Alcuin granted a leave of absence. Then he sailed across the channel, with a few of his capable students to assist him in his new work.

He came to Charlemagne's court in Aachen in 782, with the zeal of a missionary to spread the tools of learning, to lay a foundation for better morals, and to build a truer understanding of the Christian religion throughout the Empire, where civilization was just beginning to take root. He listened thoughtfully as the Frankish king explained that most of the priests in many monasteries could not even read and had to learn the scriptures by rote. How could they expect to teach others what they themselves did not know!

Alcuin's heart went out to such people. How much better his own lot had been. The monks who brought the new religion to Ireland and thence to Britain had also brought the classical studies of Greece and Rome. They saw in this no conflict with the teachings of Christianity. And he had had the benefits of these studies. As a boy he had been praised as the most brilliant pupil in the Cathedral School of York. As a young man there, he had been acclaimed a superior teacher. As head of the same school, he was acknowledged an authority on education, and people came from afar for his advice. But he knew that, besides his God-given intelligence, he had only one talent to offer — his ability to make his students *want* to learn.

Now he was forty-seven years old. He had given up his successful position in one of the most famous schools of his time to try to make a new, untutored people "want to learn." Could he do it? Here in this strange land, so-called barbarians were masters. They had accepted a religion that promised salvation, but they understood little of its deeper precepts. Even the king, for all his great desire to bring religion and morality to his people, had no real perception of the difference between right and wrong. He would crush an uprising and inflict inhuman penalties on the offenders. He did not hesitate to command punishment by death for some who refused baptism or failed to fast during Lent. Yet Alcuin sensed the deep devotion of the king and the clergy to their concept of Christianity.

The new teacher faced his class in the Palace School with interest. Before him sat Charlemagne, fair-haired and eager-eyed, broad-shouldered and long-legged, relaxed, yet with his sword still at hand. Beside him, Queen Hildegard, trying in vain to concentrate on the lesson, was obviously unhappy at being away from her family duties. She would find an excuse to drop out soon, he was certain. Brothers, sons, sisters, daughters, and other relatives of the royal family, several church dignitaries, and a number of friends were there to learn. Some were as brilliant and zealous as the king, some dull and listless, others merely curious. Most were uneducated. Even Charlemagne, despite his fine mind, had not learned to write.

What careful explanations would be necessary to make clear every lesson! What tact it would take to correct a royal ruler only a few years younger than the teacher! How could one teach with so few books — and those so deadly dull that the pupils most eager for knowledge might fall asleep as they struggled to make out their meanings?

Before each day's classes, Alcuin worked out every question he planned to ask his students. He thought through every possible answer to the questions. He used references from the few precious books that he had brought with him. He created stories to illustrate the ideas he hoped to develop. He devised puzzles and riddles to stimulate interest in facts and figures. But as usual in a school group, unexpected questions would come up. Always the king would be the most persistent in demanding answers to his "Why?" "How?" "Prove it." And as always in a classroom, a few young mischief-makers required much patient guidance before they understood that schooling was a serious matter. Fortunately, the other teachers and the students from York shared some of Alcuin's responsibilities. So he had brief rest hours during which he wrote his own textbooks.

In addition to religion, reading, and writing, Alcuin taught his most apt students the subjects that, in Greece and Rome, were known as the seven liberal arts — grammar, rhetoric, dialectics, music, arithmetic, geometry, and astronomy. These the

king absorbed eagerly. But too often he had to break
into his studies. Again and again he would be off to
crush a revolt, reinforce his borders, or inspect his
kingdom. It might be months before he came back
to the castle, the schoolroom, and to serious talks
with the schoolmaster. Most often these talks concentrated on religion, politics, and methods for educating the whole nation. Alcuin agreed with Charlemagne that the best way to unite an empire that
sprawled through most of western Europe was by
universal education. Only effective teaching and
learning could bind the people together by common
language, customs, aims, and ideals.

Schools proudly established centuries earlier had
disappeared, because the early Christians considered their teachings contrary to those of the Church.
New schools would still be suspect to the clergy, unless they were closely tied in with the Church. Both
Charlemagne and Alcuin strongly approved of
church schools. What concerned them was that
many of the illiterate clergy would become the
teachers in such schools. Charlemagne, guided by
Alcuin, found the solution in a series of proclamations. He first ordered the abbots in all monasteries
to improve their own knowledge and to keep watch
for monks who showed an aptitude for teaching as
well as for learning. This directive brought results.
Interest in education was sparked. And when the
king issued a royal edict that every parent should
send his sons to school and that each parish should
see to it that schools were available for them, the

groundwork was laid for universal state-supported
education, under the direction of learned teachers.

These proclamations were issued by Charles
himself, but the inspiration plainly came from the
great schoolmaster. Letters urging free elementary
school education for all, regardless of "whether they
were serfs or freemen," were followed up by lists of
subjects to be taught and by recommendations for
dividing the schools into classes. Thus, unofficially,
Alcuin became the first "minister of education."
Meanwhile, in the Palace School, he and his assistants continued to teach, preparing some students for
high offices in the Church, others to become rulers,
advisers to the king, administrators, and business ex-
ecutives. As for the women, they were to gain culture and so set an example for their sex.

Although born into a noble family himself, Alcuin set his own example by his humility and piety
as well as by his industry, good humor, friendliness,
and studiousness. He found that he could inspire
students with the desire to learn here as well as he
had in his own land. No one studied more assiduously than the king himself. He kept a tablet under
his pillow and nightly struggled to master the art of
handwriting. More and more he came to Alcuin for
advice. More and more he was convinced that without an educated populace no empire could endure.
And Alcuin, the skillful, stimulating teacher, opened
the eyes of his students to this fact by the best proof
possible — the change that this schooling made in
them. For more than eight years he guided his

charges on the road to knowledge, so that they might travel it by themselves. Then he sought permission from the king to return to York. He had to fulfill his promise to the Cathedral School.

This was a great blow to Charlemagne, yet he could not refuse the request of one so faithful. Before long, however, he lured Alcuin back to settle a religious controversy that had reached a deadlock. Again the deacon served the king successfully, then begged permission to retire. Instead, Charlemagne appointed him head abbot of the Monastery of Saint Martin at Tours, the most noted in the kingdom. The shrewd king was certain that here he could still seek the schoolmaster's counsel and that here the educational work would go on.

He judged correctly. Despite the age and wealth of the monastery at Tours, the number of books there was pitifully small. With the king's consent, Alcuin sent monks to York to secure more books, and soon he had another task on his hands. He became teacher, editor, and publisher. He undertook to supervise the copying of the precious volumes. Daily, during their free hours, the monks would sit in the scriptorium, bent over sheets of parchment. In the front of the room, a good reader dictated slowly and clearly from the original book, spelling out words from time to time and pointing out the necessary punctuation. As the monks wrote, Alcuin went about the room, checking the work for legibility and accuracy and discovering those monks who had particular aptitude for such copying. Thus a dozen books, painstakingly handwritten, would grow to completion at the same time. The library at Tours grew. And thence the books found their way to other monasteries.

Well known as the Abbey of Saint Martin had been, under Alcuin's direction its fame increased. Students, monks, and higher members of the clergy discovered here a center of learning where they could seek accurate information and borrow needed books. Here Alcuin's own writings on the scriptures, morality, grammar, rhetoric, and suggestions for teaching were sought. Learned teachers went out to spread the knowledge that Alcuin had revived. Students flocked to other monasteries where Alcuin's one-time pupils now taught. When the faithful abbot died in 804, several of his finest scholars carried on his work at Tours. Throughout the empire, schools continued to make progress during Charlemagne's lifetime and afterward, until an influx of barbarians from the North scourged his domain.

Today a glance at the index of any history-of-education book will show the name of Alcuin. His work lived on long after Charlemagne's empire fell apart and gradually became France, Germany, and Italy. While many people may never have heard of the kindly abbot, yet it was Alcuin's teaching in the palace court that lighted the way for learning even beyond the Dark Ages.

Vittorino da Feltre

If we follow Alcuin's light down six and one quarter centuries, we may find ourselves on a smooth, level section of meadow that adjoins a royal estate in Italy. A slender, wiry man is speaking earnestly to a group of boys ranging in age from eight to sixteen years. Suddenly he tosses his rough cloak to the ground and turns to engage one of the older boys in a fencing bout, while the others step aside and cheer them on. We are watching the quick, sure movements of Vittorino da Feltre, head of the noted court school in Mantua. Despite his gray hair, we would never guess that he is fifty years old.

His young opponent has a time holding his own, but he thrusts and parries well. Finally, satisfied that his pupil is gaining skill, the master calls a halt. His serious face lights up as he praises the progress of the lad. Next he signals two youths for a wrestling match. He looks on for a few minutes, picks up his cloak, and walks briskly across the playing field and down a tree-lined path to an imposing marble-fronted building.

When he enters, several small boys leave their educational games and urge him to see what they are doing. Vittorino observes their activities with interest. He takes the ivory letters with which the youngest have been playing and arranges them to form a word. He speaks the word and the children repeat it after him. He praises their quickness, then moves on through the rooms across the hall. He ac-

knowledges quick greetings and warm smiles from
the older students and nods with satisfaction as they
promptly turn their attention back to their studies.

Vittorino would not have believed that centuries
later educators would name him "the first modern
schoolmaster" and perhaps the greatest of his era.
Fame never entered his mind. He was born into the
Ramboldoni family in 1378, in the small town of
Feltre, Italy, from which he took his surname. He
probably attended the local Cathedral School, but
we have only a sketchy account of his youthful activities, for he himself left no written records. We
are told that he was deeply religious, equally studi-
ous, and also a leader in games with other boys.

As a youngster, he could not decide whether he
wanted to become a soldier or a priest. There
seemed little likelihood that he would ever go into
professional work, for his father, a man of respected
family background, was a notary whose earnings
barely covered his daily needs. When Vittorino was
in his teens business in Feltre picked up, however,
and his father had more clients. By the time the
youth was eighteen, college on a tight budget became possible. So Vittorino, joyfully — but wary of
the bandits who might be roaming the countryside
— walked fifty miles to enroll at the University of
Padua.

His high spirits fell when he found Padua a dismal city instead of the intellectual center of his
dreams. He was distressed to see, among the university students drawn from all over Europe, boisterous

young men rioting in the streets. He was even more shocked to discover that some of his professors were teaching for personal prestige rather than for the welfare of their students. Before long, however, he came to know other instructors, brilliant men of high ideals. He also discovered youths whose standards were as high as his own. Among his closest friends at the university was Guarino of Verona, who later made a name for himself as a great schoolmaster.

Vittorino had little time to worry over disappointments. He had to find a way to make both ends meet financially. So he undertook to tutor a few students — and had a pleasant surprise. Not only did he enjoy his teaching immensely, but his pupils made rapid progress. In fact, they did so well that more and more young men came to him for help. But he was still so distressed when he saw boys only fourteen or fifteen years old imitating the vulgar activities of crude, older youths that he made character training a part of every lesson.

He mastered his own studies easily, and after he had earned the necessary degree, he was qualified to teach in the university. Now he wanted to study higher mathematics, a course not yet included in the college curriculum. He scoured the city for a qualified tutor but found none whose fees he could afford. So he hired himself out to work as a servant in the home of a noted mathematician in return for his tuition. After six months there, during which time he surprised his severe teacher by his rapid progress, Vittorino bought the necessary books and continued his study by himself. He became so proficient that students besieged him for tutoring in mathematics, as well as in other subjects.

Still interested in helping the younger boys to improve, he set up preparatory classes for those who planned to attend the university and, remembering his own hard times, he charged pupils according to their ability to pay. His reputation for excellent teaching brought him more requests for admission to his school than he could accept. Even so, he was always on the lookout for talented pupils and sometimes took the youngest to live with him so that they would not be influenced by the rowdyism in the city.

Vittorino taught in Padua for twenty years. Then, to the dismay of his students, he decided to go to Venice, some twenty-two miles away. There he could study Greek, another subject not yet taught at the university. Within two years he returned to Padua, resumed his private teaching, and also accepted a noted professorship at the university. But after the peace and culture of Venice, the unwholesome atmosphere of Padua was more intolerable to him than ever. So in 1423, taking some of his pupils with him, he went back to Venice and opened a school.

Here he admitted boys who had the ability to profit from an education in preference to those whose parents sent them for the prestige of studying under a famous master. As in Padua, Vittorino charged wealthy parents more than those of little means. But the rich did not grumble if they discovered that their children's fees were several times as high as those of quick-witted youngsters who had scarcely enough clothes to hold out for the season. Superior teachers were hard to find.

During this period, many cities in Italy were ruled by local princes who vied with each other in making their courts outstanding. A few realized that a good school could bring honor and even fame to their cities, and several eyed Vittorino as a prize. This schoolmaster, however, was interested in working with capable young people of all classes. He had no desire to be under the thumb of royalty. Even when the Marquis Gianfrancesco Gonzaga, well-known as a wise ruler of Mantua, invited him to take charge of his court school, Vittorino's first impulse was to refuse. Still, with royal help, he might be able to encourage interest in better education for more children. This might be his chance to give young people the kind of environment that made for better learning. Whatever his reasoning, Vittorino closed his newly organized school in Venice and set out on horseback for Mantua.

Arriving at the castle, he was not impressed by its lofty towers and strong walls. He was not impressed by the magnificence inside. Instead, he was shocked to find the court filled with pleasure-seeking idlers and children who had already taken on the habits and attitudes of the grown-ups. Richly dressed, they strutted about with little respect for their companions or for adults. They showed partic-

ular disdain for teachers. One of the rudest was nine-
year-old Lodovico, the eldest son of the prince. The
child was so fat that he waddled, and so overbearing
that he already looked down on anyone beneath his
rank. This was a situation that Vittorino would not
tolerate. He refused to accept the position he had
been offered unless the pupils were set apart from
the worldly influences of court life.

Vehemently he pointed out to the prince the serious consequences for children brought up under
such conditions, and he gained his point. The prince
gave the schoolmaster a luxuriously furnished house
set in a meadow that extended to a river on one side.
Again Vittorino was not impressed. He believed in
simplicity. So he had the house stripped of its costly
finery and equipped with furniture appropriate for a
school. But he surveyed the broad acres of ground
with satisfaction. Just the thing for outdoor sports!
The house had been named La Giocosa — Joyful or
Pleasant House — and, from the first, the new
teacher made it a pleasant school.

He soon expelled the youths who had no intention of cooperating with the teachers or in the program. The rank or nobility of their parents made no
difference to him. This was an eye-opener to the pupils. Here was a schoolmaster who meant business.

It was his method of teaching, however, that
gained the respect of the pupils, and his sincere interest in them that earned their affection. Under his
guidance, the classics of Greece and Rome became
exciting. Religious writings, once dull and boring,

grew meaningful. History now showed them their place in the world. The liberal arts inspired the brighter students to delve into further studies by themselves. Music and art trained them to appreciate another face of greatness. Daily religious devotions developed a spiritual outlook. Field trips gave them first-hand experience in nature and geography. Daily athletic exercises built strong bodies. The master's insistence on good morals and manners helped them learn respect for others. Thus Vittorino carried out his conviction that body, mind, and character must develop in unison for a truly educated individual.

He also insisted on a nourishing, balanced, but limited diet for his pupils. He permitted neither idleness nor indulgence; he encouraged sports and other wholesome recreation as long as they were not overdone. He disapproved of excess of any sort, whether in work or play. He planned and organized games and play periods so that they alternated with the studies, thus keeping both mind and body in trim. And Vittorino held himself and his teachers to the same high principles that he expected of his pupils. Under this regime, fat Lodovico slimmed down to normal proportions and his arrogance gradually changed to consideration.

With the prince's permission, other aristocrats began to send their children to be educated in this busy, happy school. But Vittorino was not satisfied. He knew that many talented children could not afford a school like this. He was convinced that

Pleasant House would be a better place if youthful nobility could rub shoulders with capable young people of humble background and that the city would profit if the talents of its children could be developed. Within two years, the schoolmaster persuaded the prince to grant him a fund for educating a number of poor but bright children. As the enrollment grew, sometimes to as many as sixty children of commoners in addition to those of the court, Vittorino often covered the deficits out of his own salary. His savings dwindled but his pleasure in his pupils increased.

The master lived with his pupils, took part in their activities, and guided them according to their interests and abilities. He helped them understand genuine values and led them to think for themselves. To insure the best examples for them he selected his teachers and household helpers on the basis of their high personal standards as well as their qualifications for the work they were to do. But it was his own personality, always felt, that stimulated hundreds of students, some of whom studied under him for fifteen years, to achieve to the utmost of their capacities.

Pleasant House has been called the first modern boarding school. But Vittorino's emphasis on making lessons interesting, on teaching subjects that developed culture, on activities that encouraged leadership, self-discipline, and good character, and on practical application of what was learned may be found in every enlightened school system today, whether private or public.

Did it matter that Vittorino died so nearly penniless that his students had to pay his funeral expenses? They were the best judges of that. La Giocosa, where he taught for the last twenty-two years of his life, was the best evidence. The aristocrats who learned a lesson in democracy and occasionally remembered it were the best testimony. The heads of nations throughout the world who have come to see the need for teachers who can build zest for knowledge and devotion to high ideals in future citizens are the best proof. The progress that Vittorino's standard of teaching inspired is the final answer.

V

THREE PREACHER-TEACHERS
URGE SYSTEMATIC EDUCATION

In 1965, "more than two thousand delegates from twenty nations of the communist, neutralist, and free worlds" * convened for three days in New York City. Before this audience, a group of thirty distinguished speakers of various races and faiths, from various nations and continents, and of various ideologies discussed and debated the far-reaching possibilities in the famous encyclical letter *Pacem in Terris* — Peace on Earth — which Pope John XXIII had presented to the world two years earlier. In this letter, the Pope pointed out that mankind forms "one single family" and that every individual has certain rights as well as obligations to every other individual in the world. Among these rights are "the right to freedom in searching for the truth . . . the right to share in the benefits of culture and, therefore, the

* *Life* magazine, March 5, 1966.

right to a basic education . . ." Among the obligations is the "task of restoring the relations of the
human family in truth, in justice, in love, and in
freedom."

The purpose of the speakers, the other delegates,
and the thirty noted United States participants who
evaluated each day's session was to discover, if possible, whether in today's troubled world an active
peace might be achieved on the basis of the Pope's
doctrine. Of course, in so short a time they could
reach no definite agreement, still less a solution of
the problems that have plagued the world since it
began. But they marked the beginning of what
could be the greatest experiment in the history of
mankind.

One year later in Rome, Pope Paul VI and the
Archbishop of Canterbury exchanged the "kiss of
peace," thus taking the first step toward establishing
harmony between two religious sects that had been
in conflict for more than four hundred years. Even
this historic event could not fully mend the break;
but it cleared the first in a series of hurdles along the
road to peace between the Catholics and the Protestants. The late Pope John might have called it a first
rung in the educational ladder to his great goal —
the education of the whole family of mankind to live
in harmony with each other, regardless of creed,
race, color, economic status, or ideology.

Martin Luther

As so often happens among people who have long
been seeking a hand to guide them, it takes only one
dedicated leader to spark a great movement for the
welfare of humanity. Just so, when dissension has
long been seething in the minds of men, it takes only
one incendiary to touch off an explosion. Four centuries ago the failure to recognize man's "right to
freedom in searching for truth" touched off a confla-
gration which only today is burning itself out.

Most of us know Martin Luther as the eloquent,
dark-eyed rebel monk who tacked his list of ninety-
five statements, critical of then-current Church
practices, to the church door in Wittenberg — the
door that served as a bulletin board for the university students and also for the townspeople in that
German city. Outwardly, this monk and teacher
meant these statements as theses for debate — topics on which he and many others had disagreed for
some time. More likely, he hoped to sway others to
his convictions. But he could not have dreamed that
his act would be the lightning bolt that would split
Christianity into the Catholic and Protestant sects
— with some millions condemning him and other
millions blessing him for centuries. Surely he would
have deliberated long and hard, could he have fore-
seen the years of bloodshed, disaster, and dissension
that would follow before the split was cleanly cut.

Modern educators, regardless of their own reli-

gious convictions, recognize Martin Luther as one of
the most popular and inspiring teachers of his time.
They think of him as a crusader who made recommendations on schooling that are as vital today as
they were then. And because he thought them out so
carefully and urged them so persuasively, his suggestions set a milestone in education.

Martin Luther never forgot that he was born a
peasant. He never forgot that only a watchful Providence and his determined, hard-working father had
pulled him out of the life of drudgery that most
peasants of his day endured until death. And he
often remembered that his early learning and that of
his six brothers and sisters had been beaten into
them with the rod — at first at home and later in
school. As a grown man he recalled that his mild
and almost timid mother beat him until the blood
flowed for stealing a hazelnut. In 1483, when Martin
was born, and for some centuries afterward, the
maxim "Spare the rod and spoil the child" was practiced religiously by parents and teachers.

Eisleben, Martin's birthplace, meant little to him
in his youth, for his parents moved to Mansfeld,
Germany, when the child was less than a year old.
Here Hans Luther, Martin's father, worked at min-
ing; and the small boy did his share to help his
mother, as new babies in the family made more
work and more mouths to feed. Day after day he
picked up firewood for fuel, then returned home for
his supper of black bread and peas.

Despite this poverty, "our father, instead of making us labor with him at his own occupation, sent us to school," said Martin appreciatively years later.

Alert young Martin was eager for school but soon found it a boring chore. Sitting in the dreary, chilly classroom, he discovered that his teachers did not like teaching any more than he liked studying their dull assignments. He did not realize then that they earned scarcely enough to keep themselves alive.

Martin found Latin fascinating, but he rebelled at mastering the humdrum lessons. "I remember a day when I was lashed fifteen times for not being prepared to recite," he wrote. Even so, he learned enough to tutor some of the younger boys in the school.

By the time Martin was fourteen, his father could afford to send him away to school. So the lad and a companion, "knapsacks on their backs, sticks in their hands," walked fifty miles to a school in Magdeburg, where his teachers were Franciscan Brothers. He found the situation here little better than in his hometown, and in one way perhaps worse. Now he and his schoolmates had to beg in the streets for their food. And the handouts were meager. He had no regrets when his father transferred him to a school in Eisenach the following year.

Now for the first time, Martin discovered the joy of studying under a stimulating teacher, a man who understood young people and who knew how to make every lesson interesting. But in Eisenach, too, it was customary for the pupils to sing on the streets or in front of houses for their food. Sometimes in cold weather a kindly family would invite the boys in to get warm. Fortunately for Martin, his excellent voice marked him out to Frau Cotta, a motherly housewife. His quick mind impressed the family, and finally they invited him to live with them. The boy learned what life in a comfortable, relaxed household could be. His health improved and his personality blossomed in this happy environment. In school under his inspiring teacher, he soon became a top scholar. Three years sped by and Martin, a young man now, was ready for a higher education.

He was eighteen years old when he entered the University of Erfurt, and he delighted in the broad world of learning that unfolded before him under his professors. But his keen, critical mind did not accept everything he read or heard in lectures. He absorbed subjects that he considered worthwhile, but he did not hesitate to argue against those that seemed to him a waste of time. Socially, he was "one of the boys." He dressed as they did, joined in their fun, and out-argued the most persistent. He learned to play the lute and loved to sing to its accompaniment. Soon his room became a gathering place for a songfest, a heated debate, or just a relaxing hour. But Martin never neglected his studies. In little more than a year he earned his Bachelor of Arts degree and two years later his Master of Arts degree.

Martin could think through the basic facts in the most difficult subjects. He could weigh the pros and cons of the most controversial statements. He could defend convincingly what he considered sensible practices and he could argue fiercely against those he considered false or inconsistent. But for all his intelligence, he could not shake loose the superstitions that had seized his imagination when he was a child. The peasants of his time believed that witches, hobgoblins, and other wicked spirits were the handymen of the devil just as firmly as they believed that saints were the assistants of God. To these simple people, a great disaster like a flood or an earthquake was not the work of nature but a dastardly act of the evil one. As he grew to manhood, Martin himself ridiculed such beliefs, but during times of stress or insecurity, they flooded his mind.

Had his superstitions not interfered, Martin Luther, who was steadily gaining recognition as a fiery speaker, might have become the lawyer his father hoped for, instead of a great reformer. He had braved the usual hardships of his early youth without complaint. He had stayed on in Erfurt during the severe epidemic of 1505, when many inhabitants fled in terror. But some time afterward, while returning from a visit to his parents, he was caught in a violent storm. It came up so suddenly and the thunder rolled so ominously that to Martin it was a visitation from the supernatural. At a brilliant flash of lightning, he fell to the ground. As he lay there, he vowed to Saint Anne that, if God spared him, he would forget all worldly ambitions and become a monk.

The storm cleared, Martin returned to the university, and immediately he set about keeping his vow.

"How I astonished everybody when I turned monk!" Martin wrote in later years. "It greatly vexed my father." But in spite of his father's anger and his fellow-students' skepticism, he entered an Augustinian monastery.

The hardships of Martin Luther's youth had been bliss compared with the rigorous discipline of the next two years. But he accepted the most menial tasks, the lengthiest fasting, the most extreme self-denial happily. Now his penance was for a holy cause. He allowed himself only one luxury, the Bible. He had never seen a Bible until he was twenty years old; and the great Book fascinated him. Day after day he read, studied, and pondered over its stirring words. Even after he had been ordained to the priesthood, in 1507, the Bible, more than any other teachings, became his mentor. Within a year he was given a teaching post at Wittenberg University, in addition to his other duties.

Luther's boldness in expressing his views, his insistence on thinking facts through before acceptng them, his ability to put his ideas across convincingly, and his forceful personality made him a magnetic leader as well as an inspiring teacher. His was the spirit of the age in which he lived, the age of Columbus, Magellan, and others whose explorations into unknown territories were as daring as those of the astronauts today. Luther's ninety-five theses, posted on the door of the Castle Church in Wittenberg in 1517, quickly found their way into print. The still-new invention, the printing press, sped pamphlets and books through Europe. And Martin Luther found himself involved in a life-long controversy.

The thousands to whom he was a prophet for church reform burned with enthusiasm over his preachments. Even his opponents who called him a madman, a heretic, a vulgar blasphemer, acknowledged the power of his oratory. Unlike Socrates, he did not urge his listeners to decide for themselves. To Martin Luther, his carefully thought-out decisions were right for others as well as for himself. So effectively did he put forth his ideas that most of his students and many of the best thinkers of his time remained his disciples even after the Church had tried him and declared him an outlaw.

Martin Luther went on preaching and teaching according to his own convictions outside the Mother Church. He kept up a steady program of writing — letters, treatises, books. He even translated some of *Aesop's Fables* into German and wrote a primer for children. His translation of the Bible was superior to others of his time and is still considered by many one of the finest.

When he was no longer a priest or a member of the Catholic Church but a preacher of Lutheranism, Martin Luther married. He was forty-two years old at the time and his bride was twenty-six, a young woman who knew how to run a household frugally for a husband who was so over-generous that his earnings slipped out of his fingers almost before they reached them. In the following years, the Luthers brought up six children of their own and four orphaned children of their relatives. Martin was a devoted father to all ten and an appreciative husband to his wife, Katie — despite his occasional complaints about the troubles and responsibilities that marriage brings.

Right or wrong on the subject of religion, Martin Luther made recommendations on education that have stood the test of four centuries. He translated the Bible into German, so that the ordinary individual in his country might understand it. But he knew that in order to understand the Book, people had to be able to read it. So he wrote letters to the mayor, the alderman, and other influential persons, urging widespread education. He preached emphatic sermons on the value of education. He pointed out the need for elementary schooling for all children, girls as well as boys, the poor as well as the rich. With his usual persuasiveness, he worded these arguments so that they appealed to all classes of people.

Martin Luther built up a clear case for learning and its importance to every phase of life — the home, the town, the country, the Church. "The right instruction of youth," he wrote, "is a matter in which all are concerned." He explained the need for education to insure greater godliness, better citizenship, and more capable leadership. He pointed out that too few parents have the knowledge, time, and skill to instruct their own children; therefore schools

must be established at public expense. He emphasized that parents should be *forced* to send their
children to school. "If the government can compel
military service," he wrote, "it . . . has a right to
compel the people to send their children to school."

He recommended that book-learning and vocational training should go hand in hand — an hour or
two daily in school, the rest of the time at home
where boys could learn a trade and girls could get
training in household duties. He urged higher education for students who showed superior ability, so
that they might prepare for professional careers.
"We can take magistrates, priests, and nobles as we
find them," he said, "but not schools, for schools rule
the world." He put in a plea for good libraries,
equipped with worthwhile books. As for the teacher,
he said, "A devoted, intelligent teacher can never receive adequate reward."

When Martin Luther's emphatic pen and stirring
voice were finally stilled in 1546, other teachers
carried forward his ideas, mindless of the difficulties of that uncertain time.

Ignatius of Loyola

The "protesting" sect had to educate their children
if they were to keep pace with the new efforts of
their Catholic opponents. The Catholics were also
developing leaders who, like Luther, saw the usefulness of better schooling for young people. One

of the most dedicated and purposeful was born eight years after Martin Luther and outlived him by ten years.

Ignatius of Loyola — Inigo, to his parents — had a vastly different youth from that of the rebel of Wittenberg. He was the youngest of thirteen children in an aristocratic Spanish family who prided themselves on their noble Basque ancestry. He spent his boyhood in the home of an aristocrat serving in the court of King Ferdinand V, and his ambition was to be a great warrior.

In this period of chivalry, when education was considered too effeminate for military men, Ignatius had little more book-learning than the reading and writing his tutor had taught him in childhood. His interest in religion was as casual as that of the average high-born youth in Spain. He was having too much fun to take it very seriously. He was proud of his good looks and made up for his small stature by wearing trim, fashionable clothes and taking fastidious care of his person. He was an excellent dancer and enjoyed the attention of the ladies of the court. Outside, his boisterous high spirits more than once involved him in lawbreaking.

Ignatius went through his training for knighthood, developed into a fine soldier, and spent several years in military service. Then, in 1521, during the Battle of Pamplona in which the French fought the Spanish to regain territory they had lost to them, a cannonball shattered one leg of Officer Ignatius. Perhaps his gallant fighting impressed his captors, for they did their best to reset his bones. But their best was not good enough. They finally sent him back to the Castle of Loyola on a litter — a dangerous journey in war times. There the skilled doctors summoned by the family could not reset the bones properly. Despite two operations and intense suffering, a deformity still remained.

Ignatius spent more than a year convalescing and facing the prospect of being crippled for life. No more military service, athletic competitions, gay dancing, applause from the ladies — a dismal future for a young aristocrat not quite thirty years old.

Accustomed so long to an active life, Ignatius grew restless and irritable. With nothing else to do, he turned to reading. But there were no tales of chivalry in the castle. There were only a few books and these were on religion. Halfheartedly the invalid began to read. Gradually he grew interested. In the *Lives of the Saints* he found a whole new world. The saints were as exciting as the knights he had learned to pattern his life after. Like his contemporary, Martin Luther, he needed only one mystical incident to cement this impression into a sudden decision. To Ignatius, this experience came one night in a soul-stirring dream of the Virgin Mary and her Child. For weeks afterward its spell held him. It sealed his future.

How could he have lived so useless a life in the past, he asked himself. How could he make up for lost time and do penance for his past misdeeds? How could he do better in the future? The saints showed

the way. Instead of a coat of armor, he could wear a
cassock. Instead of weapons, he could carry a staff.
He would become a religious knight and win his
glory by a pilgrimage to Jerusalem. There he would
convert the Turks and save their souls.

Ignatius was no procrastinator. Although he was
still lame, his health and spirits had improved. Now
he threw himself into his project wholeheartedly.
He left his home and headed for a monastery. He
put on the rough garb of a hermit and gave away his
fine clothes and other worldly possessions. He
begged for food and slept wherever he could find a
place to stretch out. He deliberately gave up his
former fastidious habits and became a sorry sight,
with his red hair tangled, his beard matted, his body
unwashed, and his clothes in tatters. He spent
nearly a year in fasting and self-punishment, as penance for his sins. Then, taking only enough money to
pay his fare on a ship, he limped barefoot toward the
seaport town of Barcelona.

From there he sailed to Italy, for he needed permission from the Pope in Rome to go to Jerusalem.
In the summer of 1523, although ill and exhausted,
he joined a pilgrim ship in Venice and was on his
way to his final goal.

The month of sailing cost the pilgrim whatever
strength he had managed to retain, but his spirit
grew more indomitable daily. At last he reached Jerusalem — and disappointment. The Turks held
that city. Foreign visitors were not encouraged and
fanatic crusaders for Christianity, who might stir up

trouble, were definitely not welcome. Within two months Ignatius had to turn back.

The wayfarer must have done considerable thinking en route, for by the time he returned to Barcelona, he had made another decision. He had not given up his plan to convert the infidels, but he had discovered that in order to put his ideas across effectively, he needed an education. So again he humbled himself. At the age of thirty-three, Ignatius enrolled in a grammar school with young boys. He studied their lessons assiduously and bore their teasing and embarrassing pranks with good humor for two years. Whether he actually caught up with these classmates or whether his teacher felt that a grown man needed special leniency, we do not know; but the overage student finally received the credentials necessary to enter the Spanish University of Alcalá.

Still burning with the desire to reform sinners, Ignatius, in addition to studying, began to preach and teach his beliefs to private groups, particularly to women. His unkempt appearance and his fanatical denouncement of sin marked him as a suspicious character to the authorities, who first imprisoned him, then forced him to leave the city. Undaunted, he went on to Salamanca and set about enrolling in a college there. But he had not profited from his previous unhappy experience. Again he began his preaching to convert sinners. In a short time the authorities in this town also threw him into prison, where he was in chains for three weeks. Finally he was tried and acquitted of any political intrigue; but he was warned never to set himself up as judge and mentor of the townspeople again.

Each obstacle made Ignatius more eager than ever for a college degree. If he could not get it here and also express his convictions, he would try in France. Once more he started out on foot, begging for food and money to cover his expenses at the university. Again he stopped en route in Barcelona, where he saw former friends before continuing his journey. Then he plodded his way to Paris and enrolled in the university there. He continued to beg and dress in castoffs, but he had evidently learned to be more cautious in his preachments outside the college, for he finally earned his Bachelor of Arts degree. Still not satisfied, he took the necessary examination, passed, and received his Master of Arts degree in theology. Now he would be free to preach. More important, his sincere, intense faith in his mission won a few students to his cause. They, too, vowed to become soldiers of religion and agreed that, when they had earned their college degrees, they would join Ignatius and accompany him on a pilgrimage to Jerusalem. Nor was the promise lightly made. In 1537 Ignatius and his nine friends, with permission from Pope Paul III, were in Venice ready to sail on their pilgrimage. But again circumstances blocked their plans. War was raging between Venice and Turkey. No ships were available.

After fifteen years of devotions, study, and teaching, including the three years of waiting, forty-six-year-old Ignatius decided on a different type of

crusade. With his small band of companions, he began to work out an idea that had been growing in his
mind for some time. Why could they not recruit a
company of soldiers of religion who would carry
their teachings to dissenters and heathen wherever
they existed? If they could not fulfill their aims in
the Holy Land, then with the Pope's approval, they
would spread out and go wherever they were
needed most.

Since Jerusalem was out of reach, Ignatius and
two of his group left Venice for Rome — a long
walk that took three weeks — to seek permission to
found this new order, the Company of Jesus. And
until Pope Paul III had time to consider their plan,
the little band was busier than ever — preaching,
working in hospitals, begging to help the poor rather
than themselves, and continuing to work out their
ideas for the society later known as the Jesuit Order.

In 1540 the long-awaited permission came. Then
what an organizer Ignatius turned out to be! And
what courage the handful of original members
showed as they scattered to plant the seeds of their
ideals! As the order grew through the years, they
carried their teachings to more distant fields than
they had dared hope for — to Europe, Asia, North
America and South America.

Ignatius had been a soldier on the battlefield, a
lone crusader on an unsuccessful pilgrimage to the
Holy Land, a wanderer in search of a true mission.
He had welcomed hardships to chasten his body and
cleanse his soul. But he must have found his struggle

for the education neglected in his youth one of the greatest tortures. As he sat in a schoolroom on a bench, a grown man beside young boys, he had seen how easily they absorbed knowledge that he despaired of ever mastering. Childhood was the time for study to begin, he decided. Minds must be trained young to think in the right direction.

Although school teaching had not been included in the original program of the Society, Ignatius came to see that the new order must educate the young for their part in making the better world he visualized. For this precious responsibility they would need good teachers — teachers who could instill high ideals as well as book knowledge.

With members of the order, Ignatius worked out a system that had the precision of army training and set up a program that provided for the moral, mental, and physical growth of the students. The Company's schools would admit boys when their elementary schooling left off, probably at the age of ten. Then step by step, year by year, they would progress through graded studies suited to their age, until those who had the ability would complete the college course.

These schools would charge no fees and would be open to all boys who could meet the requirements and would live by the regulations. Training pupils in obedience to just rules and standards of good conduct, Ignatius believed, would make severe or frequent punishment unnecessary. Keeping them physically healthy would keep their minds receptive

CARL A. RUDISILL LIBRARY
LENOIR RHYNE COLLEGE

to learning. Making their school work interesting
would stimulate pupils to greater achievement. As
for the studies — in addition to religion, these
schools would teach Greek, Latin, and the liberal
arts not in conflict with the precepts of the Church.

This was a vast project for a small group of inno-
vators, but the key to their success lay in their
method of selecting teachers. No untrained teacher
faced a class in a Jesuit school. Beginners had to
prove their educational background or gain it. They
had to learn efficient methods of putting their subjects across to their classes. They had to be able to
express themselves clearly and effectively. They had
to show an aptitude for teaching. Even more impressive, for the first time the would-be teacher had to
serve an apprenticeship under supervision — a re-
quirement similar to modern practice teaching. For
the first time, too, all teachers were to be supervised
regularly.

It is no wonder that the Jesuit schools, as they
were called later, could be found in all countries of
Europe and on other continents, too, as the years
went on. It is no wonder that they survived religious
and political antagonism and even edicts banishing
the entire order. It is no wonder that today educators know the Jesuits for their successful development of the first systematic school program.

In 1556, the last year of his life, Ignatius could
count one hundred schools for advanced education
that were sending out teachers as well as leaders in
other fields. Thus in his final crusade, the first "Gen-

eral" of the Jesuits, the mystic, the fanatic, the saint, had found the means for making his vision practical.

Now, in the gradually growing parade of teachers, two religious opponents march side by side, pointing the way of learning for others yet to come.

John Comenius

Martin Luther and Ignatius of Loyola had each rediscovered many principles basic to good learning. Some of their recommendations may be traced back to teachers of wisdom as early as the Greek philosophers. But each had added his own valuable prescription for further improvement of education. Now, however, the miraculous printing press, lending wings to written words, spread the news that respected religious leaders approved this broader learning. The number of sincere, capable teachers grew, although only a few outstanding personalities rose to fame.

One who earned the right to stand beside Luther and Ignatius in a trio of preacher-teachers was John Amos Comenius. He put into print an idea about which our whole teaching program revolves today. He made clear that a child is not a miniature adult who must be forced to memorize learning-for-grownups, but a special brand of individual with a world of his own. No child is too young to learn, he insisted. But he must begin with what is already familiar and must learn through as many of his five senses as possible. During his first six years in school, his instruction should be in his native language, instead of the customary Latin; and the schoolwork must be adapted to the child's age, understanding, and ability. For knowledge must grow from the inside out if it is to be permanently captured and made a basis for higher learning.

This farsighted preacher and teacher was born in a small village in Moravia, into a family of comfortable means in 1592. Czech was their native language and their creed was that of the Unitas Fratrum, a kindly, religious Moravian Brotherhood who believed that people should live according to their highest convictions and let others do the same. These United Brethren believed in "the Bible, rather than dogma." They believed in the equality of all people and preached that simple, godly, peaceful life, devoted to the welfare of mankind, should be the aim of their sect.

As he grew up, young John Comenius found life far from simple and more and more distressing. By the time he was twelve years old, his parents and two sisters had died and their home had to be broken up. His aunt with whom he went to live frittered away his small inheritance and gave little attention to his education. He had barely four years of schooling during his first sixteen years of life.

Then he entered the Latin School in Prerov, and his two years there were drudgery from the start. Learning rule after rule that nobody bothered to explain, memorizing Latin words whose meanings he did not understand, bungling through translations without the help of a dictionary or vocabulary lists made each day a nightmare. If this work is confusing to me, an overage pupil, John thought, how difficult it must be for the young boys!

But he had set his heart on becoming a Moravian minister; so he figured out the assignments for himself, endured the monotony of his bored teachers, and finally went on to Herborn College. Here, too, he was disappointed by the cut-and-dried methods of most of his instructors. But it was here that he began his work on a Czech-Latin dictionary. Two years later he enrolled at the University of Heidelberg and made a great discovery: study could be actually thrilling.

Under the stimulating professors at Heidelberg, the young man became an enthusiastic student of theology and philosophy. Gradually an idea took hold of his imagination. If schoolchildren could have skillful, interested teachers and simply written, interesting textbooks, school could be an inspiration instead of a horror, even to the very young. By the time John Comenius left the university, he had developed the form for his dictionary and was eager to find out what this new tool for teaching could accomplish.

Already John Comenius had grown into a devout, thoughtful young man who could rise above personal problems and labor on, spurred by his convictions. During his long walk back to Prerov, the town of his Latin school days, his mind hummed with great projects. He knew that, at twenty-two years, he was not old enough to preach in the Moravian Church of the United Brethren, but he hoped to find some other way to serve. Perhaps he could write his ideas of what schoolbooks and schoolmasters should be like.

In Prerov, however, he found a better prospect, a position teaching in the elementary school run by his church. What an opportunity to try his ideas! He went to work with a will and was delighted with the results. By the time he was ordained two years later, the young minister knew that, whatever his church duties might include, he would always search his mind and experiences for methods of improving teaching. And when, in 1618, he was assigned to a prospering Moravian church in Fulnek, John Comenius rejoiced to learn that, in addition to preaching and ministering to his congregation, he also had the responsibility of supervising the schools.

During the next three years, this preacher-teacher found happiness and security in his religious and educational work and in marriage and family life. But his good fortune was short-lived. He soon became involved in a series of ups-and-downs that were to harass him for the rest of his life.

For more than a half century, the fortunes of the Catholic and Protestant sects had depended upon the religious creed of the reigning ruler. When the king was Catholic, he required all his subjects to take on this belief or leave the domain. If his successor happened to be Protestant, he expected his subjects to become Protestants directly. Occasionally, a liberal-minded emperor made some concessions, but these could not be depended on for long. Unfortunately, the Protestants themselves had not been able to settle their differences and had divided into a number of sects — Lutheran, Calvinist, Unitarian. Even these smaller groups could not agree on all religious issues and they, too, divided. In Bohemia and nearby Moravia, liberal Lutherans had broken away from the main body and organized themselves into the Unitas Fratrum or United Brethren. Their teachings were opposed by many Protestants almost as violently as by Catholics.

When Catholic Ferdinand II became king of Bohemia, the Protestants there rebelled against him and launched thirty years of disastrous, religious war that, at one time or another, involved nearly all of Europe and left a trail of plundered cities and villages and starving, homeless people. After the defeat of the rebels in the Battle of White Mountain, near Prague, in 1620, the peaceloving United Brethren became a special target of hatred.

The following year Spanish soldiers invaded Fulnek, sparing nothing, burning everything in their path. Into the flames went the labors and treasures of the young minister — his home, his church, his books, his writings. Luckily, his wife and child escaped to Prerov, where Comenius hoped that they would be safe. He and some fellow Brethren found sanctuary on the estates of sympathetic nobles. Here, although virtually in hiding, twenty-nine-year-old Comenius secretly helped other refugees, went on with his writing, and tutored the children of his protector, Karl von Zerotin.

But tragedy followed him. Within a year Comenius' little family perished in an epidemic. And within the next few years, King Ferdinand II passed laws forbidding anyone to protect or help religious exiles. Worse still, he ordered all inhabitants of his realm to become Catholic or leave. To the devout Moravian Brotherhood, giving up their religion was unthinkable. Many fled to other countries. Already the courageous minister had made one trip to Poland, seeking a refuge where his people might live in peace; and in 1628 he and a few other dedicated Brethren directed the frightened exiles to that country. Finally, Comenius and his second wife followed those who were settling in Leszno, Poland. They joined the families of the Unitas Fratrum whose ancestors had settled there in the previous century.

Immediately he set to work caring for his fellow Moravians and teaching in the school and the college of the Brethren in that settlement. He was more certain than ever that, if people were to have freedom to build a better society, they must have education. Constantly he tried out methods for making his teaching practical and for creating enthusiasm for learning. His success gained attention. His church conferred on him the office of bishop, and even Poland recognized his achievements.

Cultured, dignified, gentle but firm, genuinely

interested in human welfare, John Comenius inspired confidence wherever he went. His remarkable
understanding of young people, of school situations,
and of teachers' problems gained him increasing respect.

People listened when he explained that new scientific developments by men like Copernicus and
Kepler should be studied in school. They agreed
when he showed why the growing commerce with
the lands opened up by explorers and colonizers demanded a school program that included geography
and history. They spread the news of his activities to
other countries.

After thirteen years in Poland, Comenius was
urged to work on a project in England; but soon
after his arrival, he realized that the political situation in that country was too unsettled for educational reform. So in 1642 he accepted an invitation
to visit Sweden. When he was asked to reorganize
the educational system there, he hesitated.

"How can I leave my Brethren in Leszno?" he
asked.

"You might be able to help your fellow Moravi-
ans by working here," replied Louis de Geer, a
Dutch philanthropist with business interests in
Sweden.

Even when the man offered him an arrangement
that would help his congregation financially, Comenius still demurred. "Sweden is too far from them,"
he protested.

"Why not settle in Elbing, Prussia," de Geer suggested. "Then you will be near both Poland and Sweden."

Finally Comenius agreed. He spent almost six years working on new textbooks to be published in Sweden and devising effective methods of teaching for his patrons. Then he returned to Leszno to head the Moravian Church there.

During the same year, 1648, the long struggle between the Catholics and Protestants ended in the Treaty of Westphalia. But the joy of the exiled Moravians turned to grief when they learned that their religious sect was still banned from their native land. Despite this blow, Comenius clung to his faith in the power of education to do away with such injustice and to bring about peace for all people. His dedication spurred others to school reform. He received an invitation from a prince in Hungary to set up a new school program in the market town of Saros-Patak. Again he hesitated to leave his people; but remembering the kindness of the Hungarians to those Brethren who had taken refuge in their country, he accepted the prince's proposal and worked earnestly on this project until his patron died four years later. Then he went back to Leszno.

He found his people more hopeless than before he left. Hard as he tried, he could not think up a magic formula for replanting them safely in their native Moravia. Only the Swedish-Polish War then raging gave him hope. The Swedes were Protestants; and Comenius, long friendly to these people, en-

couraged the Brethren to support their war effort. If
they won, Moravia might be free to welcome her
own people. But the exiles had not considered the
reaction of their Polish hosts. Poland had tolerated
this outcast sect despite their despised religion.
Their rallying to the Swedish cause was treason. In
1656 Polish troops stormed into Leszno and left it in
ashes. Once more John Comenius saw his lifetime
work wiped out.

Saddened, disheartened, breaking in health,
sixty-four years old, he wandered through Germany.
His reputation as an educator had not deserted him.
Although Louis de Geer had died, his son still followed Comenius' achievements with interest. Now
he urged the wanderer to make his home in Amster-
dam and continue his work there. The educator accepted the invitation gratefully and for thirteen
years, until his death in 1670, he continued to write
and tutor students, always sending most of his earnings to his needy Brethren. At last he and his family
were secure in tolerant Holland, but they were
never to see their beloved Moravia again.

Despite his tragic life, John Comenius held fast
to his convictions. He believed that the years of
schooling could be a happy, growing-in-knowledge
period for boys and girls and he proved it, not only
by setting up systematic teaching plans for others,
but by his own teaching and in his writings. His
most amazing work is his *Great Didactic,* which develops in detail his carefully thought-out methods of
instruction, based on his conviction that "man is

formed by education," that "the child must learn to know himself, to rule himself, to direct himself to God," and that the body, mind, and soul are interrelated.

In his own day, the textbooks of Comenius made a far greater impression than his plan of instruction, for they were truly an innovation. This schoolmaster may have been among the first to recognize that "one picture is worth a thousand words," for his *Orbis Pictus* — The World Pictured — may be called the ancestor of all modern picture books and illustrated textbooks. He made the lessons in his books come alive by grouping each about some central, familiar theme, such as home life or school activities. This method of capturing interest by progressing from the familiar to the unfamiliar has proved so practical that it persists in most books for beginning readers today. Older students owe to Comenius his systematic approach to what might be called a Latin dictionary and the vocabulary lists in language textbooks.

A warring world, too, might do well to consider the plan for peace recommended by this "man without a country." He proposed a worldwide organization made up of three tribunals in each country, all working together — one headed by churchmen, one by statesmen, and one by the learned. "The tribunal of the learned would be called the College of Light," and its schools, "the workshops of light," would carry on the search for wisdom and truth. These three divisions of what might be termed an international university would work together in harmony to bring to the world enlightenment, peace, and happiness through godliness.

During more than forty years in exile, this patient, self-sacrificing crusader wrote at least one hundred books and articles, as he traveled and taught others how to teach in various European countries. His interest in youth crossed national, political, and religious boundaries. His fame at the peak of his career prompted some leaders in our colonies to suggest him for the presidency of Harvard College. This college used his textbooks; so did the early grammar schools in New England. The dedicated pilgrim's dearest wish, however — to see his Brethren reunited in Moravia — never came true. Nor could he foresee that almost three centuries later a great Catholic Pope would mirror his dream of a world reborn through education.

For over a century, except where a mere handful of professionally minded teachers tried to improve conditions, most schools continued to be drudgery at best. None seemed to remember the goal that inspired John Comenius to write: "Let us do better for our posterity." But posterity finally discovered his precepts and found them good.

When we place the achievements of this educator beside those of the other preacher-teachers in our parade, together they add a new dimension to the keystone being shaped to link freedom and progress.

VI

HEINRICH PESTALOZZI
TAPS YOUTH'S INNER WORTH

"I do not want to be the President who built empires or extended dominions," President Lyndon Johnson told Congress in March, 1965. "I want to be the President who educated young people to the wonders of the world."

These words carried by radio, television, and newspapers to the far corners of the world served to endorse the careful research, investigation, and planning that had been done for a vast program to help wipe out poverty in our country through education. One month later the President set a milestone in our history when he signed into law the *Elementary and Secondary Education Act*, which provided one billion three hundred thousand dollars for education, most of it earmarked for children in schools serving low income families.

Almost immediately wheels started rolling for a special project, Head Start, to prepare at least three hundred thousand deprived children for their first experience in school the following September. And despite numerous problems, despite the fact that nearly twice as many children as expected turned up for the summer program, the project slowly began to accomplish its purpose.

Little four- and five-year-olds, some of whom had been so neglected that they did not know how to talk to other children, let alone to adults, began to discover words with which to tell of their new experiences. Parents, some so overworked and hopeless that they accepted poverty as their permanent lot in life, began to realize that their children would now have an opportunity to lift themselves to the level of more fortunate youngsters. Even critics who clamored that federal aid to education would certainly interfere with the right of the states to handle their own school programs agreed with the President that "education is our only valid passport from poverty."

This was a magnificent vision and it has been a phenomenal undertaking. But the roots of the project trail back two centuries to the dream of a humble Swiss schoolmaster who believed that "the stature of a serf is likewise that of mankind," and that "a healthy childhood . . . is the foundation of all happiness."

Johann Heinrich Pestalozzi became prominent during the last decade of the eighteenth century when the French Revolution spilled over into Switzerland. Until 1798 the original thirteen cantons, like our early American colonies, were independent districts, each self-governing. Pestalozzi had long believed that education deserved the attention of the whole country, and for years he had tried to make the officials of various cantons recognize this need. When the country became a French satellite, organized into the "One and Indivisible Helvetian Republic," Pestalozzi saw his opportunity. He first submitted a plan for the "general and vocational education" of poor children. He followed this up by a personal visit to Aarau, the seat of the new government, where a friend, Herr Stapfer, was minister of arts and sciences.

Unaware of his rumpled hair, tie askew, and wrinkled coat, Pestalozzi stood waiting for the decision. Suddenly he started. He could not believe the words that came to his ears. Herr Stapfer was offering him the honor of setting up a teacher-training school and serving as its principal.

Slowly the small, untidy man straightened his bent shoulders. As he faced the official, his dark eyes glowing with appreciation made his pockmarked face almost handsome. He felt his confidence, so nearly shattered by years of failure, soar back on the wings of a lifelong dream.

"Will you undertake the organizing and supervising of an institute for training teachers?" his friend asked again.

Pestalozzi clasped his hands against his chest in an awkward gesture of gratitude. His words, usually blurred with worry or tumbling over each other in his eagerness, now came clear and firm. "Thank you. Thank you, kind friend — but I want to be a schoolmaster."

What prophetic spirit made this fifty-two-year-old man turn down his first offer of a position of prestige? Was it the example of his proud, shy mother, widowed so young, who brought up her children asking aid from no one? Was it the influence of his Uncle Johannes Hotz, the doctor who angrily denounced the "lordly" citizens for denying children of noncitizens the opportunity to rise above their social class? Was it the dedication of his grandfather, Pastor Pestalozzi, who not only looked after the souls of his congregation but kept an eye on their health and education, too? Probably all these, added to his own unfortunate experiences, made this idealist hold fast to his conviction that the education of a nation must begin with the young and be extended to the poor as well as the rich.

In 1746 when Johann Heinrich Pestalozzi was born, Zurich, Switzerland, was controlled by an oligarchy so firmly established that only their descendants could claim citizenship. No others in that city and no one in the outlying districts were permitted to vote or hold government positions. Still worse, the children of noncitizens were denied the privilege of attending Zurich's schools for advanced education, even if their parents could pay for it.

Although young Pestalozzi's mother was well educated and her family included a number of professional men, they lived outside the city limits and thus had no citizenship privileges. Luckily, the child's father, a doctor, could claim hereditary citizenship, which made higher education possible for his children. But Dr. Johann Baptist Pestalozzi died at the age of thirty-three, leaving his widow barely enough to feed and clothe her three children. He had, however, left her a personal legacy. He had exacted a promise from their servant, Babeli, to stay on with his wife and family, no matter what happened in the future.

Pestalozzi often looked back on the change in his life when his mother and faithful Babeli took over the responsibility of the household. His five-year-old world, just beginning to open out on new interests and activities, closed in on him. The two women comforted the three children with their love, but shut them away from other companions by their overprotectiveness.

"You must not expect to have what other boys and girls have, now that you are fatherless," Babeli would tell them. "You must take care of your clothes and not wear them out too soon."

"You must stay indoors or close to the house, so that you will not get hurt," his mother would warn.

Heinrich was happy enough in the close family circle, where he had plenty of time for daydreaming, but such life did not build strong muscles or a personality that wins other children. Taught by his mother until he was nine years old, he looked forward to school as the key that would open the door to adventure. Instead, he found a dull, fearsome world. All too soon he learned that no matter how well he understood what the teacher taught, he could never remember it word for word. He could not concentrate on the monotonous rote lessons the teacher doled out daily. He could not compete with the other boys even in the simplest sport because of his clumsiness.

During vacations he rode with his grandfather, Pastor Pestalozzi, on his rounds through the parish in Höngg, a few miles from Zurich. It was a relief to be free from the women who hovered over him so lovingly. It was fun to sit beside a wise, respected man who was not too great to answer a boy's questions. But Heinrich shuddered at the sight of poor people in dilapidated houses who had scarcely enough food to keep them alive and barely enough clothes to protect them from the weather. It was fascinating to ride through the busy streets and see people hurrying about their business. But Heinrich turned pale when he saw children at corners begging and sometimes stealing food in the markets. His grandfather explained that many orphans, and even children of destitute parents, were turned over to peasants, who would take them for their earnings or work or whatever else they could get out of them.

Heinrich swelled with pride when his grandfather visited the schools to make sure that the schoolmasters were earning their small pay. Sometimes these were set up in the shop of a shoemaker or some other workman, as an extra job to add a bit to his

earnings. The teacher would carry on his regular
work of mending shoes or weaving, while he listened to the children chanting their lessons. His
wife, her little ones, and often a dog or a cat would
wander in and out of the classroom.

Even in these schools, Heinrich saw none of the
young beggars. Schooling cost money. "Why must
they be poorer than we are, Grandfather?" he would
ask.

"Do not question the will of God," the pastor
warned.

Heinrich would pound his fist on his knee and
say, "I'll be a pastor, too, when I grow up. I shall
support the peasants. They shall have the same
rights as the townspeople."

Neither elementary school nor his years in Zurich's Latin schools inspired Heinrich with zeal for
study. But when he entered the Carolinum, the leading educational institute of Zurich, he found dynamic, liberal professors and responded eagerly.
Here he realized that he had no aptitude for preaching sermons and here he learned what education
could do for a student. He discovered that many
people who most needed or deserved good schooling
could not get it. The laws had to be changed to make
that possible.

"That's where I can help," Heinrich said to his
mother. "I'll study law."

In his zeal for reform, he joined a group of liberal college students, got into trouble for his revolu-

tionary ideas, and was disillusioned by the officials' narrow-mindedness. This decided him against law as a career. He was still searching for a vocation when he developed a serious illness.

His doctor examined him thoroughly and prescribed a change. "You must give up your studies," he ordered. "Get out-of-doors, back to nature, to a simple, healthful life. If you don't, you will suffer more attacks like this."

Back to nature! Where better than on a farm? As a scientific farmer, he might help other people to help themselves and make better lives for their children. So off to an experimental farm in Kirchberg, canton of Bern, went the student, eager to learn the newest methods. Impressed by the success of the farmer to whom he became apprenticed, young Pestalozzi soon decided to have a farm of his own where he could raise vegetables and also make a specialty of growing madder for the dyes needed in Switzerland's new cotton industry.

In the meantime, Heinrich had fallen in love. Anna Schulthess, a childhood acquaintance, daughter of prosperous, socially prominent parents, appreciated the young man's ambitions to help the masses. She mooned over his big black eyes, sure that they were a sign of noble character. Heinrich forgot that Anna was seven years older than he and felt certain that, with her fine mind and gentle enthusiasm, she would make an ideal wife. The maiden's practical family, however, considered their daughter's suitor crude, peculiar looking, ridiculous acting, and wholly incapable of providing a secure future for her.

"Prove yourself first in some respectable occupation," they told him. "Then ask for her hand."

For nearly two years the young sweethearts argued their reasons for marriage; and finally the parents consented, perhaps because their daughter was growing older and less attractive to other suitors. But they gave no dowry or promises of assistance to the thirty-year-old bride and her twenty-three-year-old bridegroom.

Such mundane matters did not trouble Heinrich. He had his bride, had bought on credit one hundred acres of arid land in Birr, canton of Aargau, and had made great plans. Within the next two years he had tilled and irrigated the soil and planted clover to improve it further. He had a large house — partly built — which he appropriately named Neuhof. Generously, he volunteered to share his scientific information with his neighbors.

But the house was too large, his neighbors grew resentful because he encroached on their property rights, his arid land improved only slightly, and repeated bad weather ruined his crops. Dreamer Pestalozzi had organized his work so poorly and kept his accounts so haphazardly that he scarcely knew where he stood financially. Within five years, even he had to admit that his farming venture was a failure. Only the help of his wife's family and a few friends enabled him to keep his house, when the creditors confiscated the other property.

The happiest event of these five years was the birth of his son Jacobi. Heinrich was fascinated by every stage of the child's growth. When the boy was three and a half years old, his father began to teach him by experimental methods. Studying Jacobi's reactions, he changed his methods when he saw that progress was slow, and kept careful records of the results. Always he was certain that practical education, begun in early childhood, could be the greatest cure for the ills of humanity.

This conviction helped him face the loss of his farm philosophically. "It is God's will, Anna," he said to his wife. "My mission is now clear. I must teach poor children how to make useful lives for themselves. I will open a Home for them. Here in Neuhof I have everything at hand to achieve this goal. Surely generous, civic-minded people will help us to get it started. And soon the children will learn handicrafts and gardening and thus will support themselves and the Home."

As if the details had been in his mind all along, Heinrich Pestalozzi developed his plan. He found a number of persons who were interested enough to contribute support for his project. In the nearby villages and along the highways he found orphans sent by their masters to beg. He found some children shifting for themselves without any supervision. He found others whose parents had put them to work as

soon as they were old enough to understand directions. To twenty of the poorest and most wretched
of these children Pestalozzi promised food, clothing,
and training in an occupation, in return for living at
Neuhof and working there during the training period. Thus began his great experiment to prove that
the right kind of teaching would make children enjoy learning and that practical knowledge would
help them develop confidence, self-respect, and the
skills necessary for earning a decent living.

In the next years, Heinrich and Anna were glad
for their over-large, though still unfinished, home.
Gradually it came to house fifty people — the children being educated, their teachers of weaving,
spinning, and other trades, and a few servants. A
conglomeration, indeed, especially at first, when the
master and his wife had to be constantly on guard.
They had to keep little beggars from slipping out to
carry on their former trade. They had to reform
those who would steal from their housemates. And
they had to create interest in those who were so lazy
that they tried to run away when faced with work.

Still worse, some parents sent their children,
dressed in rags, just long enough to get good clothes
and a little discipline, then persuaded them to leave.
Some, suspicious of a man who was fool enough to
give free schooling to other people's children, spread
gossip about him. But Pestalozzi ignored these an-
noyances.

"This is not a charity school," he would insist.
"Every individual has within him capacities of a

higher nature. Proper education can help him rise above the miseries of his environment."

To his wife he would say, "Learning is not worth a penny, when courage and joy are lost along the way. We must train these children according to their aptitudes, whether these be spinning, gardening, or some other kind of work, and while their hands are busy, they can listen as we teach them to spell and count."

The change in most of the children amazed even the master. Cringing bodies straightened, heads lifted, once-grimy faces, now bright and clean, shone with interest. But Heinrich Pestalozzi had started a project too big for one man. The children could not keep Neuhof self-supporting by their work. Only a few outsiders continued to contribute donations. Measles among the children, illness among the grown-ups, storms that battered the crops harassed the institution. Finally, Pestalozzi had to wish his pupils well and sorrowfully send them away.

Anna tried to cheer him. "Always remember, Heinrich," she said, "that in five years you have made more than one hundred children richer in knowledge and better able to live in this hard world. Now let us look to ourselves."

Indeed, this was necessary, for overwork and poverty had broken Anna's health, their frail son was too often ill for regular schooling or for work, and day after day Heinrich had to nourish his dream on a diet of bread and water. Once again he was home-bound, for his clothes were so tattered that he could not venture among people.

Folks who passed the discouraged man on the roadside turned away. "Queer he was and queer he will be," they said.

Then, for a second time, a servant became a vital force in his life. Elizabeth Naef, who had been working in the home of one of Pestalozzi's relatives, believed in his project and worried about his misfortunes. When her master died, she offered to help Anna and Heinrich.

"No, no, we cannot let you undertake this burden without pay," they told her.

But the young woman overrode their protests. She planted a garden and furnished the family with home-grown food. She restored order in Neuhof and looked after Anna. She left Heinrich free to cherish his dream.

"My whole life must be dedicated to educating the poor," he reiterated to the few friends who still stood by him.

"Then why not write out your ideas," said one, an editor of a weekly paper. "Put your plans before the people in articles, in books."

So half-heartedly Pestalozzi began a literary career, at first because he had nothing better to do. As his skill in writing grew, he decided to weave his ideas for reform into a story, so that people reading it would see how they could pull themselves out of their pitiable situations.

Using generous, energetic Elizabeth Naef as the

model for his heroine, Pestalozzi wrote the story of *Leonard and Gertrude*. In it, Gertrude, a courageous, intelligent Swiss peasant, sets out to reform her well-meaning but weak-willed husband, whose taste for liquor and poor companions have brought misery into the home. In order to stop the wily innkeeper from tempting men to drink themselves into debt, she lays her case before the new head official of the village. Meanwhile, she has developed such successful methods of teaching her own children that the official becomes interested in having all village children taught similarly. The husband, Leonard, is reformed, the wicked are punished, and the whole community finally agrees that the best remedy for the trouble in a populace is education.

The long drawn-out tale so delighted readers that Pestalozzi wrote three more volumes about the same characters. But people missed his underlying scheme to show that even the most poverty-stricken could improve themselves and their living conditions, if they had a practical education. Nonetheless, his writing brought him a meager income for seven years and considerable recognition as an author. But praise and medals do not feed the hungry; so Pestalozzi worked in various ways at Neuhof to eke out a bare living for his family.

To his delight, in 1798, after the persistent idealist had turned down Herr Stapfer's suggestion that he organize a teacher-training institute, the government agreed to set up the school Pestalozzi recommended for teaching children to become self-sufficient. But just as a location was decided on, several cantons rebelled against joining the new Swiss Republic. French soldiers hurried to put down the insurrection. The stubborn Swiss fought savagely. In revenge, the invaders burned towns, massacred inhabitants, and left desolation and despair behind them. In the village of Stans more than a hundred homeless children roamed the streets.

In his eagerness to help these waifs, Heinrich Pestalozzi put aside his other plans. Here he could do more good. His experiences with the Neuhof orphans made him sure of it. Again he petitioned the Ministry of the Republic, this time to give him the responsibility of caring for these children.

"So you still insist on uplifting poverty-ridden youth," Herr Stapfer grunted. "All right, see what you can do for the orphans in Stans. Part of a convent there will be at your disposal. You will be granted some money for running it. Good luck."

Government backing for the first time! And a project made to order for him! Brimming with enthusiasm, Pestalozzi arrived in the devastated village. The bad weather, the chill convent not yet fully rebuilt or refurnished, the hostile reception by officials of what they considered a Protestant program, meant nothing to him. Fifty children, "dirty, vermin-infested, suspicious," were his to mold into a family. Here he would create for them a home, school, church, and an opportunity for job training, all rolled into one. Here he could be father, teacher, pastor, companion to them and could work to renew their confidence and self-respect.

Pestalozzi solved many problems. When, as in Neuhof, some of the children left after they had received clothing, he quickly admitted others eager to enter. As learning difficulties came up, he devised methods for surmounting them. Interest grew. Self-assurance replaced suspicion. Surprisingly soon, most of the children showed eagerness to learn. They followed directions for sewing, mending, carpentry, and other work, so that they might help keep their equipment in repair.

Pestalozzi, laboring from morning until night with only a housekeeper to assist him, did not realize or even suspect that the Swiss government was still so involved in its struggle over unification and French intervention that officials could not bother their heads about his young orphans, now numbering eighty. He paid no attention to critics who branded his methods disorganized, disorderly, and useless play. He did not know that local politicians were just waiting for an excuse to get rid of his project — until they requisitioned the building for a hospital for French soldiers.

After five months of phenomenal success, this turn of events crushed Pestalozzi. He sent those children who had relatives back to them. The others he turned over to the Capuchin friars. Then he collapsed, critically ill. But a rest cure high in the mountains gradually improved his health. Even more quickly his dream regained its vigor. His must be a career of service to poor children.

Back he went to Herr Stapfer who again suggested that he organize and head a teacher-training school. Again Pestalozzi refused. "I want to be a schoolmaster," he said. "I want to prove how much the right kind of education can do for the poor — for our country. I offer my services free."

Stapfer had faith in Pestalozzi's genius. Other officials judged the restless little man by his careless dress, his clumsy gestures, his thick speech. They felt that he was too disorganized himself to teach children. But Stapfer persisted and finally found his protégé a position assisting a shoemaker-teacher who carried on both activities in his home in Burgdorf.

Here seventy-three children of noncitizens chanted their catechism in monotonous unison. Occasionally the master put down the boot he was repairing and went around the room to hear the children recite what they had memorized. Then he would go back to his work. Whenever the singsong babble died down, the shoemaker would shout, "Back to study, all of you. Let me *hear* you studying."

Master Pestalozzi had different ideas of teaching. He stood before his class and explained what he wanted them to learn. He let the children ask and answer questions, made them sound out words and know their meanings.

The shoemaker was appalled. This was not teaching. He was merely playing with the children, addressing a whole class at a time, *explaining* the catechism. "This man is a heretic," he complained to parents and local officials. "He will endanger our religion."

Pestalozzi had no chance to awaken these children before he was out of a job. And when his friends found him another position in a small Dame school in the same town, he held back his experiments for fear that he might be dismissed again. Still he insisted that the children understand what they were expected to learn; and he kept his teaching adjusted to each child's development. Carefully he slipped in his new ideas. Eight months later, when the pupils were tested in public examinations, the examiner's report not only commended Pestalozzi for his successful teaching methods but also recommended him for a position in the Second Boys' School in Burgdorf.

When Pestalozzi first began to teach in Burgdorf he was lodged in an old castle. Herr Stapfer's secretary, a young man named Fischer, also roomed here while waiting to set up the teacher-training school that Stapfer wanted. When the French and the Austrians clashed on Swiss soil, the government of devastated Appenzell sent the children to other cantons where they could find care and safety. Some thirty in charge of a young schoolmaster named Krüsi made their way to Burgdorf and before long a num-

ber from other pillaged cantons joined them. The
children were taken into the homes of kindly families, but their teacher was housed in the castle.

All three of the men in the castle were keenly interested in educational practices and they found
much in common. Fischer soon took another position, however, leaving Pestalozzi to eventually organize the normal school. He and Krüsi, who had
been teaching in different sections of Burgdorf, decided to combine their classes. They secured the
necessary permission and were granted part of the
castle for their school. As more and more children
sought admission, the town allowed the teachers to
use the whole castle, rent free, and also paid them a
small salary.

With Krüsi as his assistant, Pestalozzi was able to
extend his work, train several teachers, plan the
normal school, and devote some of his time to writing. His new book, *How Gertrude Teaches Her
Children,* brought his ideas on teaching to the attention of many people. More important, in this school
he had freedom to put his ideas into practice. No
more rote lessons in arithmetic without understanding it. Instead, the children placed pebbles side by
side and made their own rules for adding and sub-
tracting. No more memorizing the alphabet before
attaching meaning to the letters. Instead, the children placed letters together to make syllables and
words. Then only would they chant what they had
absorbed to further fasten it into their minds. Such
exercises were fun, instead of boring.

As the number of pupils in the institute grew, the story of Pestalozzi's amazing teaching methods spread. And when the normal school got under way, more and more student teachers came for a course of three months. Visiting educators, convinced that here was something that could revolutionize learning, often stayed on to study the procedures. They marveled at the ease with which the children mastered knowledge in an environment so free that it sometimes mounted to clamor. But the eagerness of the pupils when they undertook a project was inspiring. Most unusual was the evidence that there was no need for punishment. The children listened to the schoolmaster "as to a wise father." The teachers turned to him "like loyal sons" and put his methods into practice.

Still the master was not satisfied. In this school some parents paid for their children's education. It was not the answer to his dream. "An industrial school for poor children has been your ambition," he kept telling himself. "Remember it."

Now was the time, Pestalozzi decided, to set up a school for orphans and destitute youth. Surely he could get enough financial support from so many interested citizens and friends. But when it came to giving money, people were less generous than they were with praise. So the schoolmaster found another way to achieve his goal: he admitted more non-paying students to Burgdorf Institute.

Once again Heinrich Pestalozzi was running a household of more than a hundred persons; and the number of visitors who came from other countries steadily increased. Some stayed on as instructors. Pupils educated in the institute often took positions there. An Austrian lad, Joseph Schmid, who entered when he was fifteen, had developed into a master teacher of mathematics. Observers gasped at his skill. Building on Pestalozzi's methods, he could put advanced mathematics across to the children more easily than the average teacher could drum ordinary arithmetic into their heads. But the faithful Krüsi and several of the original staff were the bulwark of the faculty.

During this peaceful time at the Burgdorf Institute, political controversy raged among the cantons. Pestalozzi was considered important enough to be sent to Paris as one of the delegates to confer with Napoleon in an effort to keep the cantons united in a central government. He took this as an opportunity to promote his ideas on education. But Napoleon was too busy for ABC's. He refused to see the delegation. So Pestalozzi passed out circulars explaining how a system of education sponsored by the government could cure the evils in the nation.

But Switzerland did not maintain its central government much longer. Napoleon decided that a weak and divided neighbor was to his advantage. The following year, 1803, the individual cantons regained their independence.

Burgdorf Institute in the Canton of Bern lost its government support, and the officials reclaimed Burgdorf Castle on the pretext that they needed it for the home of their prefect. Luckily, Pestalozzi was now famous throughout Europe. Other cantons offered to provide him with a building and equipment if he would establish his school in their territory. The schoolmaster did not want to leave the area where his experiment had taken root, so he accepted offers from two nearby towns, Münchenbuchsee and Yverdon, and transplanted his students and faculty first to Münchenbuchsee. But once again his impulsiveness brought complications. He agreed to combine his school with a successful industrial institute nearby that was conducted by Philipp von Fellenberg, a long-time acquaintance who had followed his methods enthusiastically. All too soon he realized that he could never work with a man who demanded hardheaded business efficiency in running a school. So he left that project in the hands of Fellenberg and moved on to Yverdon, taking with him the nonpaying students, in whom he felt the deepest interest.

At Yverdon a huge old castle was already being repaired for the promised facilities. Pestalozzi was delighted. The spacious rooms were ideal for indoor classes. The broad courtyards were perfect for outdoor work, sports, and play. The master and his staff set up a daily schedule with specific periods for instruction, study, work, recreation, and rest. Here he could train body, mind, and spirit simultaneously.

People who had marveled at Pestalozzi's success with the Burgdorf Institute were even more impressed at Yverdon. Many more came to study the unusual system the master had developed. The school often housed more than two hundred students at one time and the teaching staff grew proportionately. Visitors stayed on for weeks, months, and occasionally for several years. Friedrich Froebel, who based many of his own successful practices on those of the Swiss educator, visited Yverdon in 1805, and was amazed at the "alive" atmosphere among the students and faculty. He called Yverdon "the holy city of education." A Frankfurt physician who took his sons to Yverdon was so impressed that he interested his own city in the new methods. An important French official whose sons studied under Pestalozzi published a glowing account of his work. The king of Prussia and the czar of Russia sent students to train as teachers. John Griscom, a professor in the American college now known as Rutgers University, returned home to write: "The success of the methods depends upon the personal qualities of the teachers." A New England educator, William C. Woodridge, wrote: "The institution of Yverdon is crowded with men of every nation, even agents of kings and noblemen, who come to learn his principles."

Pestalozzi had again undertaken a task too big to encompass personally. The master was so busy experimenting with new methods and explaining his work to the steady stream of visitors that he had to leave the running of the institute to the teachers. Despite the efforts of Krüsi and a few other faithful workers, feuds broke out among the faculty. Young

Schmid continued to be Pestalozzi's pride and joy, although other teachers recognized that the mathematical genius had let his success go to his head and was now working for his own glory. Several excellent teachers left Yverdon and opened rival schools that attracted a number of the institute's pupils. In 1810, Schmid went back to Austria to open his own school. As gossip about the dissension spread to the outside, more parents withdrew their children. The inspectors who had originally rated Yverdon so highly now decided that the children needed more religious instruction and stricter discipline. Financial support dwindled and debts piled up. Loyal teachers contributed out of their own small earnings but their help was not sufficient.

Some years earlier Pestalozzi's son Jacobi had died; and his wife joined her mother-in-law for a time. But Anna was the steadying influence on her husband and on the staff at Yverdon. When finances there were at their worst, she came into a small inheritance that helped stave off the creditors. Schmid, whose good management and superior teaching had been sorely missed, was called back. He, too, paid some of the debts out of his own savings, and he began to reorganize the institute in a more practical, businesslike way.

The staff could relax again. Visitors continued to stream to Yverdon. Then in 1815 seventy-seven-year-old Anna Pestalozzi, whose health had been poor for years, died. At first the shock seemed too great for her husband to bear, but very soon he forgot his sorrow in new plans for his school. He leaned ever more heavily on Schmid, who gradually became the evil spirit of Yverdon Institute. Although the teachers acknowledged the brilliance of his instruction and his devotion to his own work, his domineering manner antagonized them and also the other help. Even elderly, faithful Elizabeth Naef, who had married Krüsi's brother and was now a widow, refused to stay on under Schmid's domination. But not until Krüsi, loyal for sixteen years, and Niederer, another teacher who had been a mainstay of both Burgdorf and Yverdon, deserted did Pestalozzi collapse under the burden of grief. Again he had to be taken for a rest cure in the mountains. During his absence more teachers left and the few who remained continued their feud.

But Heinrich Pestalozzi returned. Seventy-two years old, now he nourished a vision of opening an institute for poor young people whom he could eventually train to teach children of poverty understandingly. A number of people who still believed in his genius subscribed generously to a fund for this enterprise. In 1818 the dream became a reality. Pestalozzi opened a "poor" school at Clindy, not far from Yverdon. Success again. The small number of pupils originally enrolled increased steadily. Paying students begged admission. Interest of outsiders continued. But within a year this project, too, had grown too much for the elderly schoolmaster. Reluctantly, he agreed to Schmid's suggestion that he combine Clindy with Yverdon.

As the arguments, complaints, friction, and debts mounted during the next few years, Pestalozzi wanted to transfer the institute to Neuhof. But even his most loyal friends saw that he was too old for another venture. "Educating the nation through your writings should be your aim now," they urged. So in 1825, he closed the doors of Yverdon behind him. Still longing to teach, he took Schmid and four students to Neuhof where his grandson and his wife lived. Until his death two years later, the schoolmaster continued to write, welcome visitors, make the rounds of the village schools, and speak at meetings.

"I lived as a beggar that others might live as men," wrote Heinrich Pestalozzi. He never realized that he personified his own belief that "he who bears the interest of humanity in his breast is sacred."

Today more than ever educators echo the kindly schoolmaster's credo that children learn by doing, that they must *understand* what they are expected to learn, and that in order to be understood new ideas must grow out of their own experiences. Teachers are increasingly aware of the fact that "freedom is the ability to govern one's self," and that freedom and progress forge ahead side by side.

In a world fraught with hazards that a man like Pestalozzi could never have imagined, thinking people fervently agree that "the salvation of the world is civilized humanity," and that the highest type of education must be directed toward this end. In a world where millions of people are still oppressed and where other millions are free for the first time to explore their own potentialities, thinking people agree with Pestalozzi that "the stature of a serf is likewise that of mankind." The farsighted statesmen who launched the Anti-Poverty Program were heeding the Swiss educator's warning that "hundreds of wretched men are lost for the want of someone who might rouse them to a sense of their inner worth."

VII

FRIEDRICH FROEBEL
CHANNELS THE SPIRIT OF PLAY

Less than a generation after the elderly Pestalozzi opened his school for the poor in Clindy, Switzerland, a woman watched another aging man lead a troop of little children from a shabby farmhouse in Bad Liebenstein, Germany. As he arranged them in circles, his tall, angular figure and jerky motions made him look like a scarecrow in the farmyard. The stables, pigsty, and cowpen in the background added to the picture.

"The 'Old Fool,' they call him," muttered a passing native of the popular vacation village. When the man began to prance about with the barefoot children, his long gray hair lifting with his movements, his clothes flapping about his lanky body, he looked every bit a clown.

As the fashionably dressed woman approached,

he turned from his charges, his pride in them still shining in his eyes. "They can play by themselves now, Baroness," he said, before she could apologize for interrupting him. Then straightway he began to tell her about the success of his classes for training women to teach young children. "Women do especially well with the little ones — better than men, who lose patience too soon," he said.

The woman, Baroness von Marenholtz-Bülow, was stirred by the man's fervor as he went on, "I say again that the destiny of nations lies far more in the hands of women . . . than in the possession of power. . . . In their children lies the seed corn of the future."

The man, Friedrich Wilhelm August Froebel, might have added that his own destiny had been molded by the lack of a woman's affection in his childhood. He could not remember his own mother, who had died when he was nine months old, and he remembered his father more for his absence than for his presence at home, in Oberweissbach, Germany. In the early 1780's a busy pastor looking after some five thousand parishioners in a half-dozen villages had little time to look after his family, and the servants in the motherless household had little time for the toddler. Fortunately, the child's brothers, especially Christoph, took young Friedrich under their wings for the next few years, until Pastor Froebel decided to remarry.

At first the boy enjoyed the care and attention of

his new mother; but when her own son was born, she focused all her affection on the infant and brushed her small stepson aside. The child, the boy, the man with a mission always carried the scar. He could not shake off the poignant loneliness of the four-year-old, constantly ordered to play outside, yet always warned not to go beyond the yard to join other children. He could not forget the sessions when his father tried to teach him to read. He wanted so much to please that every mistake he made tied his tongue and clouded his mind.

In the village school, only arithmetic came easily to Friedrich. He hated being forced to learn rules. He closed his mind to the daily scoldings. He learned little and earned a reputation for stupidity, mischief, and untrustworthiness. When he was reported to his father for one offense or another in school or at home, nobody bothered to find out whether the fault was really his. Why tell the truth when grown-ups would not believe him anyway. He began to hate school, church, even his family — all but his brother Christoph.

Friedrich saw this brother only on rare occasions now, for the young man was studying theology at the University of Jena. His few visits home brought exciting times, especially when his father flew into a temper over the new liberal ideas Christoph tried to discuss with him. What a wonderful place the university must be — to dare let its teachers and students think differently from Pastor Froebel!

Gradually Friedrich's loneliness lifted in a dream. If I could go to the university, he thought, I'd show them that I'm not so stupid as they say.

When he grew older he wrote: "A picture of my mother often came to me." Her spirit always seemed nearby whenever his need was greatest. Why else did her brother, Uncle Hoffman, come to visit when his nephew was ten years old and "the despair of the rest of the family as well as himself"? What else but memory of his mother helped her brother persuade Pastor Froebel to let his problem son go to Stadtilm for his further schooling?

The five years in Uncle Hoffman's home were a revelation to Friedrich. The gentle clergyman treated the lonely boy like a normal lad. He made his nephew feel that he was filling the gap left by the death of his wife and his only child. The mother-in-law who looked after the Hoffman home in Stadtilm gave the boy freedom to wander at will in the garden, to roam the nearby valley, and to wade in the brook with the other children. Here he met kindness and understanding for the first time. The child was in classes with forty others of his own age and soon caught up with them in his studies. Here he practiced so hard that "his schoolfellows could tolerate him as a companion in their games." Here he learned to love nature. "Perhaps I'll study agriculture someday," he said to his uncle.

The world became beautiful, the family a haven; school brought new interests; church, unexpected comfort.

When Friedrich returned home at the age of fifteen, his yearning to study at the university no longer seemed a farfetched dream, for his uncle believed in his ability. But he still dared not mention his ambitions, for his stepmother had convinced her husband that this son was not college material. Yet when Pastor Froebel apprenticed him to a forester for two years, the youth performed his tasks enthusiastically. His master, Friedrich wrote in later years, was "a good forester but a poor teacher"; so the young apprentice spent his spare time reading the books at hand, making a map of the area, and collecting plant specimens.

Still hoping to continue his studies when his apprenticeship was over, Friedrich turned down the forester's request that he remain another year. Disappointed, the man wrote Pastor Froebel a report filled with complaints about his son's conduct. As usual, the family did not trouble to find out whether the accusations were true. Even after Friedrich proved them false by producing the satisfactory testimonial the forester had given him before he refused to stay on, his parents would not believe this son worthy of further education.

Friedrich remembered his father's warning when he began his apprenticeship. "Do not come to me with any complaint, for you will not be listened to. You will be considered wrong beforehand."

"The wings of my mind were bound again," Friedrich wrote later. He turned irritable, surly, and uncooperative.

By this time Christoph had completed his course for the ministry, and a second brother, Traugott, was studying medicine at the University of Jena. Seventeen-year-old Friedrich had almost lost hope of attending any college, when an urgent letter from Traugott arrived. He needed money at once; and the only one free to take it to him was Friedrich. What an opportunity! Eagerly the youth set forth, his spirits soaring higher with every mile he walked.

When he arrived in Jena the very sight of the university thrilled him, filled him with plans. Almost immediately he sounded his brother out. "Now that I'm here," he ventured, "if I had the money, I could stay."

"So you could," Traugott agreed. He looked thoughtful, then said, "You should stay — at least for the eight weeks left of this summer term. I'll write Father and ask him."

To Friedrich's delight, his father agreed; and the next two months seemed to prove his ability to continue. Then once more his mother seemed to stand beside him. The trustees of her estate allowed him to have part of a small legacy from her so that he could continue at the university. This amount would cover his entire course and living expenses. He enrolled immediately and threw himself enthusiastically into his work. By the following term, he was doing so well in botany that he was invited to become a member of the Natural History Society. Although he was supposed to be scheduled for practical subjects, he soaked in the ideas of German philosophers like Immanuel Kant and Johann Fichte, whose theories on knowledge, reason, learning, and education were constantly discussed in classes and on the outside.

At midsemester the young student, appreciative of his brother's help in making this wonderland of education possible for him, lent Traugott part of his college fund. Confident that he would get it back when he needed it, Friedrich forgot about the loan until his own money ran short. By this time, however, Traugott had left the university. He could not or would not return any of the money. So Friedrich asked his father for help and met with a firm, "No!" The trustees in charge of what was left of his legacy held fast to the letter of the law and also refused him money.

What was he to do? He would not leave the university where for the first time he felt equal to other young men. Instead, he let his eating-house bills run on and hoped that they would be covered somehow.

In young Froebel's day, falling into debt was a crime; and before long he found himself in the university prison. Certain at first that his father would come to his aid, Friedrich read, studied, and thought about his future. As the days dragged on, however, he grew depressed, bitter, and critical of everything around him. Not until nine weeks later did his father have him released and then only at a price. He agreed to pay the debts, provided that Friedrich would give up all claim to his rightful share in any future inheritance from his father's estate.

My stepmother's doing, the young prisoner

thought, so that her own son may have it. Well, let him keep it.

So for the third time Friedrich showed the poor business sense that hampered his progress the rest of his life — in lending his brother money without assurance of getting it back, in running up bills he could not pay, and in forfeiting his legacy. He told himself glumly that now he was glad he lacked the money to continue at the university. He could not face the shame of his prison record there. He convinced himself that he no longer approved of Jena, that the courses were disconnected and impractical, and that without the brilliant minds of a few professors and scholars, it would be a deadly, dismal place. He was done with formal education.

Frustrated and disheartened, Friedrich began an odyssey of four years, going from job to job — as a caretaker on a farm, a clerk in a forestry office, a bookkeeper, an overseer on a large estate. During his father's last illness, he helped out willingly, glad that they were understanding one another at last. Still nothing satisfied him. But when his Uncle Hoffman died, leaving him a small legacy, the wanderer forgot his grievances against higher education. Now I can prove my uncle's faith in me; now I'll study architecture, he decided. So again young Froebel traveled the shining road of hope.

This time he went to Frankfort, where he planned to study under an architect while waiting for the credentials necessary for enrollment in the university. Almost immediately he began to question himself. "Is this new vocation my true business in life?"

"No!" his ever rebellious inner tormentor seemed to shout. "Already you are dissatisfied."

During the waiting period, Froebel met Anton Gruner, one-time pupil of Pestalozzi and now headmaster of the model school in Frankfort-on-the-Main. They found much to talk about, especially after the younger man had visited the experimental school. As doubts about his aptitude for architecture increased, Friedrich poured out his indecision to Master Gruner. "What do you advise?" he asked. "Can I use this vocation for the betterment of mankind?"

Gruner shook his head. "Your very doubts give the answer. Architecture is no vocation for you. You should be a teacher."

"Teaching as I have known it is all wrong," Froebel protested. "Besides, I need a practical vocation."

"You'll find teaching practical enough," Gruner said. "Become a teacher. We want one in our school. Say you agree and a place will be yours."

Still Froebel hesitated — until news arrived that the credentials he needed for admission to the university had been lost.

"It is an omen," he told Gruner with a sigh of relief. "I will be a teacher."

"From this moment on," Friedrich Froebel wrote, "I determined to give up my life wholly to education."

In Anton Gruner's school, at the age of twenty-three, the young man faced his first class and felt as much at ease with them as though he had been teaching all his life. Thirty-five boys from nine to eleven years old soon became a family to him. At this same age he himself had crossed the bridge from the chill indifference of his home to the warm, stimulating life at Stadtilm. He must do for these children what his uncle had done for him.

But Friedrich realized even then that teaching is a many-sided career. He wanted to learn how best to teach. Where better than at Yverdon, under the great master who had helped make Gruner successful. So within three days after making this decision, he was on his way, eager to prepare himself for his chosen vocation.

"What I saw at Yverdon was to me at once elevating and depressing, and also bewildering," Friedrich told Gruner, after he had spent two weeks at Pestalozzi's institute.

He approved of the rigorous life that the teacher and pupils led. He liked the absence of luxuries and formal dress, the simple food, and the friendliness between the teachers and students. He was fascinated by the kindly little man whose work had become the watchword in the educational circles of Europe. He was amazed at how much could be accomplished when children were grouped according to proficiency instead of by age. He was astounded to see the ease with which the young could grasp arithmetic. But as he headed for Frankfort again, he pondered over why the institute troubled him. A lack of unity among subjects, he decided. I can improve on that.

Back in Anton Gruner's school, Friedrich Froebel began at once to set up a course of study that would coordinate all the subjects. The boys responded eagerly. Physical geography, especially, became alive to them. In the girls' school, where he also taught some classes, he met the same enthusiasm. Froebel's classes in the model school became outstanding.

"A fine teacher," people said of him, after witnessing the public examinations. "This is how subjects should be taught."

Toward the end of the year Froebel again became restive. This school is too big, he thought. Pupils here live by rules and schedules. Children should be *led* to knowledge. Learning must grow within them until each advancing step comes naturally.

Still searching for his particular niche, now in the field of education, Froebel left the model school, determined to learn French. To earn his expenses he undertook to tutor three boys. His French lessons proved a failure, for he had never been able to learn grammar; but his tutoring more than met the approval of the boys' parents who urged him to continue with them.

"Only on one condition," he told the parents. "The boys must be entirely under my care. We must

live a simple life in the country. I want to correlate
their learning, so that it becomes truly a part of
them."

Under their tutor's guidance, the young pupils
led a rural life. They gave up luxuries, did their own
gardening, went on hikes to learn natural science
firsthand, and devoted such hours to study as
seemed needed. By the end of the year, Frobel decided that they were still not getting a well-rounded
education; so with their parents' permission, he took
them to Yverdon. In 1808, he and the youths became
pupils in the old, rambling, four-towered castle, now
teeming with more than two hundred students and
forty teachers, all inspired by the great Pestalozzi.

Tutor Froebel had not expected the steady
stream of visitors who came from near and far to
learn, to teach, and often to criticize. A wonderful,
stimulating place and a dedicated master, he concluded; but "it is growing into a circus." Why cannot
Pestalozzi's instructors integrate what they teach
and thus educate the *whole* pupil? Perhaps it is because each teacher is sure only of his own subject,
instead of understanding every course taught in the
school.

Despite this faultfinding, Froebel remained at
Yverdon for two years, teaching as well as studying.
Then he decided that he needed a broader background of subject matter. So he took his three
charges back to Frankfort, where he continued to
tutor them for some months. Then he went on to
Göttingen and enrolled in the university there to

study languages. His difficulty in mastering grammar still hampered him, but he plodded on until his funds ran low.

His mother's spirit again seemed to direct assistance his way. Her sister died, leaving nephew Friedrich enough money to make him financially secure for a short time. Eagerly he resumed his studies, now in the sciences for which he had an aptitude and in which he did well. But as usual, he grew discontented with the instruction and moved on. He went to Berlin to study under a famous mineralogist and earned his living by teaching in a small institute in the city. With the inspiring teacher at the University of Berlin he could find no fault.

At this time, Berlin was in a turmoil of revolt against Napoleon's domination of Germany; and soon Froebel's inner tormentor began to rebel, too. How could he expect to make a career of teaching young people and inspire them with a love of their country, unless he, also, stood ready to defend their Fatherland. He answered with his usual eagerness for change.

He gave up his studies and joined a well-known army corps. There he met several young men who agreed with him on the need for improving education. Two Berlin University students, Wilhelm Middendorff and Heinrich Langethal, became his particular friends. Between raids and skirmishes, they spent much of their spare time in discussion. "Man and the education of man was the subject that occupied us long on our walks," Froebel wrote in his autobiography. Army life gave him a new perspective. "Freedom cannot be bestowed upon us. . . ." he concluded. "Every individual has to free himself by the help of educational influences."

After the Peace of Paris in 1814, Froebel worked for a time in the Mineralogical Museum of Berlin. But the desire to teach tugged at him. Ideas for improving on Pestalozzi's methods filled his thoughts. Once more he began to tutor; and as he listened to his two young pupils, he thought of his favorite brother Christoph, who had contracted typhus while caring for French soldiers and had died of the disease. He remembered the letter from Widow Froebel begging advice on how to educate her three sons. My brother's boys are fatherless, he said to himself. I should be looking after them as he once looked after me. With that idea uppermost, Froebel started for Griesheim, where the widow still lived in the parsonage — a plan growing in his mind as he went.

On his way, he stopped in Osterode to visit a third brother, Christian, a successful manufacturer in that town. Here his plan developed. He persuaded Christian to let him take his two boys, aged six and eight years, to Griesheim, so that he might educate them with Christoph's sons.

Arriving at the parsonage, Friedrich greeted his sister-in-law with his usual impulsiveness. "I will be a father to your sons," he promised. "Here I will open a school for them."

Straightway, Froebel rented a house and named

it The Universal German Institute. Then with his five nephews as a class, the thirty-four-year-old schoolmaster began to develop his theories. Punishment can bring out the worst in children, he remembered from his own childhood; so there must be no formal discipline in my school. I will "use all talents and dispositions, and bring each learner into his proper place." Here there must be a "giving and taking . . . between the teacher and pupil." I must integrate the subjects I teach, so that each child will enjoy a well-rounded schooling.

Froebel kept in mind his two army friends and their interest in education. Before the institute was fully under way, he persuaded handsome, well-spoken Middendorff to join his venture. Langethal was not free to come, but he sent his eleven-year-old brother to be educated under his friend. Widow Froebel was as enthusiastic about the school as her brother-in-law. When she had to give up her home in the parsonage, she sold whatever property she owned and bought a small farm in Keilhau, a hamlet ten miles away. It would make an excellent site for a school and a new home, she was sure.

Despite the fact that a shack and a tumbledown farmhouse were the only buildings on the land, Froebel was delighted with the spot. The distant hills, pungent pine trees, and rugged countryside were just the thing for healthful living. The hundred native inhabitants of the village were so primitive in their customs and so thrifty in their habits that "they handed down clothes from one generation to another." This fit perfectly the first step in the school's program — to train children in simplicity. Inspired, the two teachers prepared the farmhouse for occupancy, and within two months they sent for Mrs. Froebel and the six boys.

A year later, when army friend Langethal arrived to take his brother home, Froebel enticed him to give up his plans to enter the ministry and to join the staff at Keilhau. The new teacher, with his excellent education and cultured background, was not only a personal asset to the small school but he brought with him five pupils from his hometown. Now Keilhau was a going institution. But a famine plagued the area. There were more mouths to feed and less to feed them with. Expenses piled up. When funds finally gave out completely, Widow Froebel came to the rescue. She sold her silver and secured enough money to save the institute.

Thus far, Friedrich Froebel had taken women's help for granted. He believed that women should be grateful for the education of their children. But his sister-in-law remembered his promise, "I will be a father to your sons." When she learned that he had proposed marriage to a wellborn, well-educated young lady whom he had met in Berlin, fury boiled up in her. She packed to leave. She demanded that her ungrateful brother-in-law return the money she had invested in the school. She threatened to sell the Keilhau property, to take the boys out of the school, and to go to the magistrate for her rights.

To silence the angry woman, Froebel officially bought the property, promising to pay for it in the future. He was content to see her go as long as her bright sons remained with him. His agreement to pay he forgot as soon as she was out of sight. He continued his courtship, married attractive Wilhelmina Hoffmeister, and brought her and her adopted daughter to Keilhau.

The bride knew little about household duties and still less about how to deal with young boys. Yet she braved the unaccustomed poverty and high-spirited youths because her husband was so engrossed in his project. She had no means of helping financially, however. Within two years the school faced disaster.

Fortunately, prosperous Christian Froebel decided at this time to move his family to Keilhau and join his brother's venture. In his enthusiasm, he invested his whole fortune in the institute, a transaction which paid off the most pressing debts. Luckily, too, Christian's wife was an excellent manager and her three daughters assisted willingly. During the next six years, the school population grew from twenty to sixty pupils. New buildings were erected and several more teachers were employed. The project seemed headed for success.

"Keep in tune with nature" was its motto. Study natural science in the mountains and nearby forests. Eat just enough for necessary energy. Wear light-weight clothes — the older, the better. Let your hair grow as nature intended. Train the will with proper habits, and train the mind with studies appropriate to each individual.

The inhabitants of the village had something to say about this program. "This queer establishment is a disgrace," they reported to the magistrate. "We do not want these long-haired, strangely dressed people among us."

Froebel had to yield to the law and order the boys to have their hair cut. He had to direct them to wear clothes like those of the native children whose hand-me-downs looked chic beside the makeshift garb of his pupils.

Then the staff began to complain that Froebel was too rigid in his ideas, that he had no business sense and would take advice from no one. Christian Froebel soon realized that putting his money into the hands of his brother, without asking any security, had only complicated the institute's financial problems. A teacher named Herzog found fault with the whole setup. He pointed out that the master had no regard for the teachers' opinions, yet he threw most of his own responsibilities on their shoulders. He accused Froebel of deliberate dishonesty in dealing with his sister-in-law. He filled her sons' heads with such tales of injustice to their mother that the boys left the school. This damage done, Herzog went off to Jena, spreading scandal about the Keilhau Institute as he went. Mistrust grew. Christian's money was gone. Pupils were being withdrawn. Creditors were clamoring daily.

"Ah," sighed Froebel long afterwards, "many a day I would slip out the back door and leave our tactful Middendorff to calm their anger."

During the next few years, pupils continued to drop out until only five remained in the school. Finally the others in the family had to remove Friedrich from authority and take over the management of the institute themselves. Fortunately, Middendorff's nephew, a businesslike, practical young man named Barop, had joined the staff. He undertook the task of setting up the school on a sounder basis.

Undaunted, Froebel set out to seek assistance from people who had once appreciated his ideas. Now they saw him as a failure, however, and were reluctant to throw good money after bad. Even so, the schoolmaster had his devoted following, especially among the women. At this time, the mother of the boys he had taken to Yverdon offered a solution. She introduced him to a "composer and science enthusiast" who listened to the story of his ambitions with interest.

"Come to Wartensee," he said finally. "My Swiss castle will be at your disposal for a school."

So in his fiftieth year Friedrich Froebel began his Swiss career. In a short time, he came to the notice of the people in the area. Some praised his work but others had a far different opinion. Conflicting tales trickled back to Keilhau, and Barop was sent to find out how the work was progressing. He saw the shortcomings of the situation at once.

"This is no place for a school to grow," he said.

"It is so run-down that repairs would cost a fortune. Even if you could persuade the owner to remodel the castle, you would have trouble with the people in the village. Already they are calling you a heretic."

As the men sat in a tavern discussing this sorry state of affairs, three merchants joined the conversation. "We have just the place for you," one told them.

"Come to our town, Willisau, in the canton of Lucerne. We need a good school," said another.

Froebel, indignant and obstinate, refused to consider the proposal. Even Barop was skeptical, until a delegation sent by twenty prominent families persuaded them to transfer their school to Willisau. With the terms settled, Froebel returned to Keilhau to bring his wife to her new home.

In Willisau, forty pupils responded quickly to their new schoolmaster's methods, and he responded happily to their confidence in him. But the clergy could not understand his strange ways of teaching. They warned the people to beware of the man. Nevertheless, the twenty families continued to believe in Froebel's ability to improve on the hit-or-miss methods of the former teachers.

"Work on," the mayor advised. "Then prove yourself by a public examination of your pupils' achievement. Let the people see what you can accomplish."

The public examinations proved successful far beyond anyone's prediction. From seven in the morning until seven in the evening the whole town witnessed the children's proficiency. A final hour of games and exercises impressed the observers as much as the superior academic achievement.

The school at Willisau had opened in May, 1833, and Friedrich Froebel became a principal "at the call of the people" for the first time. In two years he gained such recognition that he was asked to organize an orphanage at Burgdorf, serve as its director, and also give three months' courses for teachers — projects formerly dear to Pestalozzi. To Froebel this was the pinnacle of his achievement. But the orphanage gave him his greatest inspiration. Working with young children for the first time, he discovered that he had an instinctive affinity for the preschool age.

Watching the little orphans, so serious in their play, Froebel realized that here was a "natural activity." Games, songs, dances, storytelling, sandpile play, when properly channeled, could guide the development of the *whole* child. If only he could find some simple way to direct this natural activity toward systematic learning! "My mind pursued this vision endlessly," he told friends years later. "Then one day, while watching the children in a simple game with a ball, it came to me in a panorama. A ball is a toy to a small child. Why not a cube also? And a cube may unfold into a variety of forms that could build concepts. Educational toys! I would call them 'play-gifts.'"

From that hour on, idea after idea based on the

interests of the preschool child blossomed in Froebel's mind. He devised educational toys, tried them
out on the Burgdorf orphans, and exulted in the results. Bursting with creativity, he decided that he
wanted to devote all his time to his project for this
age level. He would need a place where he could be
free to experiment. Keilhau was the answer. But efficient Barop, who had finally cleared that institution
of debts, knew the improvident Froebel too well to
get involved in his daydreams again. He refused
permission, but he did secure a renovated powder
mill in Blankenburg for the experiment. Here the
fifty-five-year-old schoolmaster began his greatest
enterprise.

Now he was occupied every moment. He gathered a group of peasant children for his pupils. He
took part in their play and created more educational
toys. He wrote out methods of using the ball, cylin-
der, cube, paper cutouts, and old-time circle songs
— as ever greater possibilities filled his thoughts.

Teaching, traveling, and lecturing in important
cities like Dresden and Leipzig helped him spread
his ideas among people interested in education, but
brought little support for them. Still he was happy in
his new mission.

When his wife died in 1839 life became mean-
ingless to Froebel. Faithful Middendorff took the
grieving man to Keilhau, certain that the best medicine would be seeing teachers at work educating
young people. The cure proved miraculous. Within
a month, Froebel was back with his little pupils in

Blankenburg, so busy that he had no time to think of his personal problems. Sure that his skeptical audiences were missing a great educational opportunity by not endorsing his project, he sought new ways to convince them. Perhaps if he could think up a simple, arresting name for this preschool class, it would help. But how could a few words encompass this great idea? Day after day he muttered, "If I could only think of a name for my youngest born!"

It came to him one fine summer day as he looked down from a hilltop on the green gardens growing in the valley below. He stood there, face glowing, eyes shining, and shouted, "I have it! *Kindergarten* shall be the name of my new institution."

June, 1840, the festival time honoring John the Baptist and the four hundredth anniversary of the invention of printing, brought also the annual birthday party for all the children of the Blankenburg and Keilhau institutes. So Froebel planned a joint celebration in Blankenburg. In a speech that opened the festivities, the father of the new infant in education officially named his brainchild *kindergarten*.

Now the educator began to spend his meager legacy from his wife on advertising schemes to support his new program. As usual, he was soon deep in debt, and Barop had to come to the rescue. But as long as he could continue his work, Froebel was content to let others worry about his financial problems. With his own small printing press and Middendorff's help, he already had his ideas printed, illustrated, and packaged; so he started on a tour through Ger-

many to arouse interest in the kindergarten. Then he
went back to Keilhau, where Barop grudgingly let
him organize a class for training kindergarten teachers.

At the age of sixty-seven, this persistent innovator decided that he needed a school entirely his own,
not only for working with preschool children but
also for training teachers who could carry on his
work. The rundown farmhouse at Bad Liebenstein
seemed an ideal solution. Perhaps at this time any
other place would have pleased him, for the elderly
educator had fallen in love with a woman thirty
years his junior. And tall, graceful Luise Levin, who
had first worked at the Keilhau Institute as a kitchen
helper and later studied under Froebel, appreciated
his genius and returned his affection. The family at
Keilhau stormed at the idea, however, chiefly because they considered Luise inferior to Friedrich
and to them. But the enamored schoolmaster shut
his ears to all arguments.

To Bad Liebenstein, the popular watering place,
came Baroness Bertha von Marenholtz-Bülow.
Wealthy, intelligent, cultured, and progressive, the
woman grew curious about the eccentric man whom
the natives called the "Old Fool." After visiting his
school several times her curiosity turned to interest.
She observed Froebel's experiments with his play-
gifts, "the little figures made of sticks, the paper cut
in squares and folded to show the relationship of
surface and geometric forms," and pondered over
the philosophy in his book, *The Education of Man,*

fascinated by the possibilities in his innovations. She, too, began to study under Froebel and before long was devoting most of her time to promoting the kindergarten idea. Influential in social and political circles, she soon brought his achievements to the attention of persons prominent in educational activities. She also secured a small hunting castle nearby where he could carry on his work in more pleasant surroundings. Here the broad, tree-shaded grounds became a schoolroom and play-yard for the children in nice weather. Indoors there was plenty of space for classes; and a large hall made an excellent gallery for exhibiting the master's play-gifts, his *Mother Play-Songs,* and his other books.

Despite the disapproval of the Keilhau family, Friedrich Froebel's marriage to Luise Levin was a gala affair that promised him permanent happiness at last. But trouble clouds never failed to hang low when security seemed assured for the dedicated master. Widow Froebel's sons like avenging spirits hovered nearby. Carl Froebel, who had become known as a "revolutionary," was also training teachers and was advertising his own school in brochures competing with his uncle's. One reached the attention of officials who promptly labeled it atheistic. As a result, Friedrich Froebel's work, too, came under suspicion, and in 1851 the government of Prussia ordered all kindergartens closed.

The shocked educator was inconsolable. Almost overnight he became an old man. His friends tried to intercede for him. The baroness conferred with the top government commission, urging that the edict be set aside. Her plea was ignored. She refused to yield; and when the officials admitted that they could not prevent people from setting up classes in their homes, she found families who were glad to co-operate in the project. Thus the work went on and created more interest than ever.

For his seventieth birthday, Froebel's young wife, friends, teachers, and pupils staged a party that made the anniversary a crowning occasion. Among his many gifts, the most moving was an orange tree from the children. Its leaves, buds, flowers, and fruit dramatized Froebel's favorite example of the various stages of man.

Not long afterward, when he was addressing a meeting of the National Council of Teachers in Gotha, the tremendous applause told him that his greatest idea was finally taking hold. Back home again, the indomitable crusader for educating youth from the cradle must have felt free at last to leave his work wholly in the hands of others. Within two months, on June 24, 1852, Middendorff and Luise, with many villagers, stood in the rain beside his grave.

Their tribute to this creative schoolmaster was not one of lengthy, futile mourning. Instead, they went forth to carry on his work. Middendorff, during his one remaining year of life, moved Froebel's kindergarten materials to Keilhau and continued to work there. The baroness, who in 1860 joyfully saw the edict against kindergartens rescinded, worked for forty years to interest people in classes for preschool children. Luise Froebel trained children and teachers in her own kindergarten in Hamburg, Germany, for the rest of her life — nearly a half century.

"If three hundred years after my death, my method of education shall be completely established, according to its ideas, I shall rejoice in heaven," Friedrich Froebel had said to the baroness, when he recovered from the shock of the government's ban on his classes.

He did not dream that within four years one of his students would carry the German kindergarten across the seas to Wisconsin in the United States. He did not foresee that within eight years an American woman inspired by his work would set up an English-speaking kindergarten in Boston; that twelve years later one of Luise Froebel's students would establish a kindergarten in New York City; and that in 1873 another would open, in St. Louis, the first public school kindergarten. But if he could see the hundreds of thousands of little children today happily learning through play in cheery public school kindergartens in every part of the civilized world, surely his joy would resound throughout eternity.

VIII

HORACE MANN
WINS THE CASE FOR "COMMON SCHOOLS"

In the spring of 1837, when Friedrich Froebel gave up his other enterprises and established his kindergarten in Blankenburg, Germany, he inscribed his name in the history of education. On June 28 of the same year, on the other side of the Atlantic Ocean, Horace Mann was considering a change that could affect the course of his whole future. He had agreed to serve as secretary of the first State Board of Education of Massachusetts if that position were offered to him.

Carefully as he had considered this proposal, Horace Mann still had some doubts as he paced the floor of his Boston law office. Had he been right in promising to undertake this new venture?

Like the German innovator Froebel and the Swiss reformer Pestalozzi, the American stood at the crossroads when his life was more than half over. Like these educators, he had grown up in the kind of environment that made him yearn to improve conditions for the children in his country. Unlike these two Europeans, however, the American had steadily gained recognition in his chosen career and was respected as an excellent lawyer, an honest politician, and a citizen devoted to the welfare of the new republic.

Giving up his profitable law practice and the honor of serving as president of the Massachusetts Senate was not what troubled the senator now. It was the meeting the next day. The State Board of Education would vote then to extend to him a formal offer of the new position. So said board member Edmund Dwight, his friend who had discussed the proposal with him several times during the past weeks.

Horace Mann's deep-set gray eyes grew anxious as he asked himself again, "Ought I to think of filling this high, responsible office? Can I adequately perform its duties?"

Lawyer Mann had to weigh all sides of the question. To do so, he turned back the calendar almost two centuries. In every era, great thinkers had believed education to be the best cure for the social, religious, political, and economic woes of the world. The hardy colonists who had brought the customs, traditions, and culture of their mother countries to America agreed that their children had to learn to read in order to understand the Scriptures. Forward-looking leaders in more than half the colonies had established laws requiring that all children be taught at least to read and write. Massachusetts, by the middle of the seventeenth century, had set fines for people who failed to obey these regulations.

Horace Mann did not need to ask why officials had permitted such laws to be ignored for years. He knew the excuses. The Revolutionary War had sapped the energies and finances of the people. Many teachers had to serve in the army and, without them, most of the schools closed. The growth of industry in the early nineteenth century seemed to make the rich richer, the poor poorer. In the average family, even young children had to earn whatever they could to help meet expenses. Some needy parents sent six-year-olds to work in factories, at times for as long as sixteen hours a day. Others put their children to work on farms or hired them out to prosperous families. They could not spare them to go to school. Besides, some schools were closed because teachers would not work for a few dollars a week in districts where overage, oversize, unruly pupils made life almost unbearable for them.

People who were prospering hired tutors or sent their children to private schools. Only a few worried about the masses who could not afford such luxuries. Gradually the scattering of the "common" or free schools came to be known as "pauper schools" and were humiliating to parents and children. No wonder the education of the average person during Horace Mann's youth was little more than second-grade level.

In 1796, when Horace Mann was born, the Constitution of the United States was just nine years old and George Washington was still President. On a small, barren farm in Franklin, Massachusetts, Horace learned the hard facts of New England life. In order to secure the bare necessities for existence, the whole family had to share the work. In the young republic, educational opportunity was still for the privileged. Even parents like Thomas Mann and his wife Rebecca, who both recognized the value of a sound education, could not look forward to giving their five children more than the smattering of schooling available in the district school of their town. And when Thomas Mann died, leaving the children to be cared for by their mother alone, hopes for a better future grew dimmer.

Horace was thirteen years old when this tragedy struck the family, and he doubled his efforts to help in every way possible. During the warm weather the tall, gangling youth did more than a man's work on the unprofitable farm. In winter, besides their other chores, he and his brothers and sisters helped their mother braid straw for the hat-makers in the area. Part of their small earnings paid for the books they had to buy for their brief sessions in the district school.

Thinking back thirty years, Horace Mann murmured, "How I longed for an education! But until the age of fifteen, I had never been to school more than eight or ten weeks in any one year."

The Mann children gladly took advantage of the limited schooling offered in Franklin. In the square, unpainted, one-room schoohouse, the pupils nearest the fireplace drowsed in the early-morning burst of heat, while those on the far sides of the room shivered in the raw chill of stale air. Six hours a day they sat on hard, backless seats, trying to memorize the lessons assigned and waiting their turns to recite them at the teacher's desk. The taller pupils shuffled to ease their cramped legs, while the smallest dangled their feet some distance above the floor. As for the teachers, they were good people and well-meaning, but they had little knowledge of the subjects they tried to teach and no training whatever for teaching.

Horace probably learned more from the small library donated by Benjamin Franklin to the town named after him than from his public school teachers. He had easy access to the books, because for four years his father was treasurer of the library. Judging by modern standards, the library's 116 books, most of them old histories and theologies, must have been pretty dull reading. But to young Horace they showed a panorama of the past and "lent wings," as he said, to his "boyish castles in the air" that always "had reference to doing something for the benefit of mankind." Years later his reverence for books moved him to write, "Had I the power, I would scatter libraries over the whole land, as a sower sows his wheatfield."

College education for the thoughtful, earnest youth was an undreamed of luxury until a traveling schoolmaster named Samuel Barrett settled in Franklin for a time and advertised his tutoring service for a fee so small that even Horace could afford it. This excellent teacher recognized the young man's ability and encouraged him to prepare for college. Would there be money for such education? There might be, for Horace could draw on a small legacy from his father to pay the yearly tuition of twenty dollars at Brown University. For the rest he would work whenever he found the opportunity.

The glorious prospect brought forth all of the student's energy. For six months he studied every spare minute of the day and late into the night. And when he took the entrance examinations at the university in Providence, Rhode Island, he not only passed but entered as a sophomore. How he worked during the next three years! It was worth the effort, for he was graduated at the head of his class in 1819.

Twenty-three-year-old Horace Mann had decided to become a lawyer, so he entered an apprenticeship in a law office in Wrentham, Massachusetts. Within six months, however, Dr. Asa Messer, president of Brown University, offered him a position tutoring in the college. Here was an opportunity to share his education with other young people — and to earn a salary of $375 a year besides. It was also an opportunity to continue his friendship with Dr.

Messer and his family — and to be big brother again
to the youngest daughter, twelve-year-old Charlotte.
Horace accepted the offer and for the next two years
he threw himself wholeheartedly into his teaching.
His sound background of information, his enthusiastic presentation of each subject, his clear-cut explanations, and his willingness to let his students
express their own opinions inspired them to reach
for the ever higher standards he set. And he met
their exuberant rowdiness with his usual good humor.

Despite his success in teaching, Horace Mann
still aspired to a legal career. He left the university
and studied for two years at the law school in Litchfield, Connecticut. In 1823 he was admitted to the
Massachusetts Bar, after which he entered an office
in Dedham as a practicing lawyer.

From the first, Horace Mann's dignified bearing,
his ready wit, and his sincerity impressed people. As a
speaker he held his audiences spellbound. As a lawyer, he refused to take any case that he considered
unethical or unworthy. His integrity won the confidence of his fellow citizens in the district and in
1827 they elected him to the Massachusetts House
of Representatives. The fact that he was one of the
youngest ever to hold that office did not keep him
from speaking his mind.

Here was his chance to realize his dreams for
serving humanity. With the fervor of deep conviction, Mann spoke out in defense of religious liberty.
He hammered home arguments in defense of the still-
new, still-feared railroads. He argued that instead of

competing with the canals and stagecoaches, they would unite the whole country and bring about better business conditions. He described the pitiful state of the mentally deranged people housed in jails and almshouses so movingly that he stirred the conscience of many listeners. Even doubters hung on his words, thought them over, and often came to see their wisdom.

During these years, Horace Mann continued his friendship with the Messer family; and Dr. Messer, although no longer connected with Brown University, followed the achievements of his former student with pride. Gradually Horace began to realize that visits to his friend's house seemed dull and flat when Charlotte was not there. Suddenly he discovered that she was no longer a charming little girl but an attractive, tantalizing young lady, whose dark eyes and warm smile drew him to Providence every time he had the slightest excuse for the trip. With success in his profession assured and affection in his heart growing greater every day, Horace found the courage to propose marriage to Charlotte. Impatiently he waited through a long making-up-of-mind period, but she finally set the wedding date. When she became Mrs. Mann, his happiness lightened every task he undertook. Unfortunately, as she grew older, Charlotte was rarely in good health for any long period of time. Even the tender care of her husband failed to help. In less than two years he was a widower.

Without his lovely young wife, life turned drab

for the congressman. Dedham, where so many of his dreams had grown into reality, held only painful memories for him. So he gave up his home and his career in that district, moved to Boston, and began his law practice anew. He crowded out his bitter thoughts with long hours of hard work. The only successes that brought him genuine pleasure were those that helped to improve the lot of the common people.

Horace Mann could not remain an unimportant figure long. People recognized his earnestness, his fearlessness in speaking out against unprincipled schemers, and his insistence on just laws. They elected him to the Massachusetts Senate. Now, successfully launched as president of that lawmaking body, he stood on the threshold of another career.

Horace Mann raised his silver-gray head and straightened up to his usual erect posture. His eyes brightened and his face grew serene as he considered his achievements. In court, his fiery speeches had won four out of five of his cases. As a member of the state legislature, he had helped secure the appropriation for building, in Worcester, the first mental hospital in the United States. He had championed prison reforms that would rehabilitate prisoners instead of merely shutting them away from society. He had firmly opposed the teaching of religion in the schools. As president of the Senate, he had signed James Carter's bill creating the new State Board of Education. Could he do as much for

mankind, if he gave up politics for the untried secretaryship?

The offer of the position was an honor, but even
more it was a chance to test his faith in "the improvability of man." As a lawyer he could secure justice
for a certain number. As a senator he could sponsor
legislation to promote better social conditions. But
in this work for the State Board of Education, he
could help every child to improve, not only for his
own benefit but also for more intelligent citizenship
in the growing republic.

Horace Mann accepted the position when it was
formally offered to him the next day. At the age of
forty-one, he resigned from the Senate, closed his
law office, and began his new career.

"The path of usefulness is open to me," he wrote
in his personal journal after he had made his decision. But where to begin was the question. First he
had to learn as much as he could about the educational program already established in Massachusetts. Where would be the best place to do this
thinking? Back home in Franklin, of course. So he
assembled the few available books and pamphlets
on the subject, wrote to the directors of town and
district schools for more information, and settled
down to find out what his new duties should be.

He soon discovered that they would be many
and varied. The original school laws had been made
on a town basis. In 1647, for example, Massachusetts
required "every town with fifty inhabitants to hire a

schoolmaster and arrange for his pay." But as the
settlers gradually moved from the coast and scattered to inland areas, their children could not reach
these schools. In some sections, traveling teachers
went from one makeshift school to another, teaching
for a few weeks in each. Gradually small independent schools were set up in the villages. Each was a
one-room building with one teacher for all the children between the ages of six and sixteen.

Most of the teachers were men, sometimes mere
youths who had been educated in similar schools. If
they could read, write, do simple arithmetic, and
keep some kind of order, they had the required qualifications for the job. The few women teachers usually taught only in the summer and were paid only
half as much as the men. Standards varied in each
school and the books used in each building were mediocre and inadequate.

Secretary Mann decided that one of his first
responsibilities was to awaken the people to the
need for more and better "free" schooling. So at the
end of August, he set out on a lecture tour through
Massachusetts, traveling on horseback and by stagecoach. From the start he found that he could expect
harsh criticism as well as praise for his efforts. At
times he was depressed by the bitter opposition of
an audience — and even more depressed when only
a few people showed up to listen. Just as often, however, he was elated to realize that those who questioned him most skeptically were beginning to understand that they had a responsibility to children

other than their own. Invariably, he gained the life-long support of some people. In Cyrus Peirce, principal of the Nantucket High School, he lit the spark of dedication to universal education.

For three months Horace Mann continued his campaign and whenever possible he visited the schools in each area. The tiring tour strengthened his conviction that the scattered district schools needed to be organized into a state system of education. During these and his later travels, Secretary Mann inspected at least eight hundred schools. He reported that most of them were "close to the roadside, poorly ventilated, unsanitary, with no pumps or wells for water," and at some distance from houses where they might get any. He found that barely one-third of the townships "maintained schools for the benefit of all inhabitants," as the law required. Every district was independent and handled its educational program pretty much as it saw fit. Most of the state's fifty-six hundred teachers lacked any training for teaching, showed little understanding of children, and still less "aptness to teach."

In a lecture on education, Secretary Mann said to his audience, "I have seen many schools in central districts of rich, populated towns, where each seat connected with a desk consisting of an upright post jutting out of the floor — the upper end eight or ten inches square — without side arms or back rests." Dramatically, he described schools where rain that dripped through the ceilings drained through holes

in the floor and schools so cold in winter that ink
froze on the pens. He told of teachers who imprisoned mischievous youngsters in "dark, solitary
places" and of others who punished talkative
children by "bracing their jaws open with a piece of
wood." Some schoolmasters kept pupils in order by
making offenders "hold heavy weights until they
were ready to drop from exhaustion." As for flog-
gings, they were the accepted penalty for failure to
master an assignment, as well as for misbehavior.

If only we could combine these hit-or-miss district schools into one organized school system, with
the state and the towns each sharing the cost and the
supervision, we could correct most of these evils,
Horace Mann told the Board of Education members
and influential friends when he returned to Boston.
But how could he spread this idea? Speeches were
all very fine, because they gave the personal touch,
but the secretary wanted to get his observations and
recommendations to the people in writing, so that
they could think them through. An educational magazine might do it, he decided. So he added the publi-
cation of the *Common School Journal* to his mount-
ing number of responsibilities.

He had to plan for lectures several times a week,
answer many letters concerning his work, plan and
follow up school programs throughout the state, and
prepare annual reports for the Board of Education
and the legislature.

How he labored over the first report! He knew
that it could determine the support his future recom-

mendations would receive. What an unhappy picture of the school situation in Massachusetts he had to present! How would the Board react to it? He need not have worried. His forthrightness and devotion to the project shone through every criticism and brought him praise and increased respect.

One of the secretary's major problems was securing teachers for the "common schools," the public schools of his day. "Moulding young minds and young hearts is the noblest task that can be entrusted to a man or an angel," he believed. Only qualified teachers who would do their best to raise the standards of teaching could ennoble the task. Where were they to be found?

Horace Mann was not the only educator who worried about this situation. For years James G. Carter, a teacher, a member of the state legislature, and now a Board member, had been unsuccessfully pressing for laws that would establish teacher-training schools in Massachusetts. Horace Mann thoroughly approved of Carter's recommendations and found other progressive citizens who favored the idea. But could they convince the legislature to allot the money for it? Suddenly, like a miracle maker, Edmund Dwight volunteered to contribute ten thousand dollars for such training schools, provided that the state of Massachusetts would give the same amount for the purpose.

Full of enthusiasm and hope, the secretary presented the offer to the Board of Education. Three months later, the legislature voted to appropriate

the matching ten thousand dollars for the establishment of three normal schools for a trial period of
three years. Horace Mann was delighted. This was
his first major conquest in his new educational program.

Meanwhile he had launched another project. He
had been investigating the library situation and was
distressed to discover that in the whole state only
twelve libraries were open to the general public.
There were, of course, college libraries and private
libraries for the use of their own members, but these
were closed to outsiders. The state should appropriate money to set up libraries in the common
schools, Mann decided. Dared he request it? He did.
And to his delight, he received a small amount for
books.

As soon as the news came out, new problems
arose. Publishers, authors, and literary agents besieged the secretary, urging him to recommend their
books for the schools and libraries. Unfortunately,
he found few that met his standards. Several books,
among them one by a minister, were promoted by a
very persistent agent. But when Horace Mann read
the ghastly tales of children, shrouded and in coffins,
who would pay dire penalties after death for misbehavior on earth, he was disgusted and said so. The
agent remembered Mann's speeches against religious teachings in the schools. Now his refusal to
buy these books for libraries and classrooms proved
him a godless man. "He is an atheist," the agent
fumed to anyone who would listen. This slander

stirred up a tempest in a teapot, which simmered down before long. But those people who remained enemies never lost an opportunity to harass the secretary.

In selecting locations for the normal schools, Horace Mann had to be careful not to offend persons who urged him to recommend their unoccupied buildings. In choosing principals for these new institutions, he had to be especially tactful. But the educator skirted the trouble spots safely. For the first teacher-training school he rented a vacant academy in Lexington and persuaded Cyrus Peirce of Nantucket to serve as principal.

Getting the building ready and the rooms furnished and securing the necessary books and equipment for the classrooms required long hours of planning and supervision. But at last the opening date was set for July 3, 1839.

Eagerly the secretary and the principal awaited the first students, but good fortune deserted them when they needed it most. A veritable cloudburst deluged the area on opening day. Only three drenched young women braved the storm to take the entrance examinations. By fall, however, the number had grown to twelve. But the results of the examinations! Instead of capable young people of high school ability, most of the enrollees needed instruction in reading, spelling, and basic grammar. Poor Cyrus Peirce found himself principal, teacher of all subjects, building supervisor, fire-stoker, and odd-job man that year. Nonetheless, the first public nor-

mal school in the United States had been launched;
so Horace Mann went happily on to his other duties.
Few people knew then that he had sold his law library to help furnish the school.

During these years, Horace Mann wrote in his
personal journal, he averaged fifteen hours of work
a day. Yet life had not been all job and no social contacts for the widower. When he moved to
Boston, he had taken lodgings in a boardinghouse
where a group of congenial people lived. Here he
found much in common with several men and also
with two young women, Elizabeth Peabody and her
sister Mary, who conducted a small private school in
the same house. For a time Mr. Mann was able to
forget his troubles in relaxing company at meals and
in the evenings. With the well-educated teachers he
talked school, religion, politics, and philosophy.
Even after he moved again, he continued to visit the
stimulating Peabody sisters as often as possible. But
if he ever suspected that each young lady secretly
hoped for a closer relationship, he kept that thought
closely hidden within himself.

Secretary Mann had little time to think of ro-
mance, for his work demanded full attention. In
1840, all three Massachusetts normal schools were
under way — the first in Lexington, the second in
Barre, and the third in Bridgewater. Since these
were on trial for the first three years, he had to be on
hand frequently to observe their progress.

He also had to battle opposition to them. A new
governor stood for economy and proposed some

alarming changes. Do away with nonessentials —
revoke the appropriation for normal schools and libraries, eliminate the State Board of Education and
the secretary's position. The old district school setup
was good enough.

Many people applauded the governor's stand.
Some felt that compulsory education infringed on
their rights as parents. Some, who sent their children
to private schools, objected to paying taxes for the
common schools. Factory owners saw a cheap source
of labor gone if all children were required to go to
school. Influential leaders, like ex-governor Everett,
Edmund Dwight, and the Connecticut educator
Henry Barnard, resolutely backed Horace Mann. The
recommendations were discussed hotly, neither side
giving an inch. Finally the controversy came up for
debate in the legislature.

Again Horace Mann need not have worried. The
majority stood firm for laws that would provide free
improved education for all children in common. And
when in 1842 the state legislature voted six thousand
dollars to continue the normal schools for three more
years, and fifteen dollars a year for each library, the
secretary knew that his long hours of work had paid
off.

During this period, Horace Mann had discovered that Mary Peabody had come to share the
affection he had so long held sacred to the memory
of his beloved Charlotte. For ten years both sisters
had followed Mr. Mann's work with interest. Brisk
elder sister Elizabeth championed each of his inno-

vations enthusiastically. Gentle Mary quietly helped him keep his notes for speeches, reports, and manuscripts in good order and occasionally wrote articles for the *Common School Journal*. The educator valued the friendship of both women. What prompted him now, in the midst of planning a trip to Europe, to propose marriage to Mary was his secret. But Mary, writing of her joy at his proposal, left no doubt about her long-time devotion to her fiancé. As for Elizabeth, if her sister's engagement brought any disappointment to her, she covered it and rejoiced that "dear Mr. Mann" would be her brother-in-law.

There was no long waiting period for the widower's second marriage. Within five weeks Mr. and Mrs. Horace Mann were on the *Britannia* sailing for Europe. Yet even during his honeymoon the bridegroom remained an educator. While others devoted their holiday to sight-seeing, entertainment, and shopping, the Manns used much of their time to visit schools, observe methods of teaching, inquire about teacher training, and read educational publications. They also visited hospitals and looked into prison conditions. They found many situations worse than in their own country; but they were impressed by the "intelligent, . . . kind, conscientious teachers" in the German schools. They liked, too, the rapport between the teachers and pupils in Scotland.

Back in Boston, the secretary decided to include his observations on European schools in his *Seventh Annual Report*. Although he had traveled at his own expense, he had taken six months off for the trip, so he owed this information to the Board. With Mary now always on hand for reminders, suggestions, and translations of the German pamphlets he had collected, he felt truly inspired. When he turned in his report, he was sure that it was one of his most enlightening surveys. He never dreamed that it would offend the teachers. But it set off a storm of controversy.

Massachusetts educators considered their schools the best in the nation. And here was the secretary of the Board of Education, who should have been upholding his hard-working teachers, comparing them unfavorably with foreign teachers! Thirty-one Boston schoolmasters rose up in anger and published their *Remarks on the Seventh Report,* denouncing its author.

Lawyer Mann replied to these *Remarks,* and he took this opportunity to review the progress he had made during his seven years on the Board of Education. He reminded the "Thirty-one" that they themselves had complained bitterly of the deplorable school situation before 1837, and he pointed out how much still needed to be done. So what began as bad publicity probably goaded many teachers into experimenting with newer teaching methods and spurred the citizens of Massachusetts into giving more thought to their school system.

During this time, the battling secretary had home problems to think of, too. In February, 1844, his first son was born. Papa Mann was proud of tiny Horace but he could not help worrying about this new responsibility. He was nearly forty-eight years old. Would he live long enough to guide this infant into successful manhood? By the time his second son was born, he was more intent on giving both little fellows a happy, well adjusted childhood than on what could happen in the future.

These years had brought other changes. The Barre Normal School had been moved to Westfield. The one at Lexington was being transferred to West Newton. Horace Mann, convinced that a small town would be better for his children than the city, decided that West Newton would be an ideal village for a home. With his mind made up, he lost no time in carrying out his plans. By Christmas of 1846, the Manns were installed in their dream house, built according to the careful design of its owners.

How delighted they were with the spacious rooms, the porches, the gardens, and the outdoor freedom for the children. And how pleased they were to be able to entertain visiting educators comfortably in their own home during the next two years.

Then in February, 1848, John Quincy Adams, who had served a term as President of the United States and had later been elected to Congress in Washington, died suddenly. The news was a blow to the whole nation. But to Horace Mann the loss brought another crisis. He was asked to replace Mr. Adams for his unexpired term in the House of Representatives.

To leave his new home, his wife, who was expecting her third child, and his two small boys would be a hardship. But how could he cut himself off entirely from the educational program that had shown so much promise during his twelve years as secretary of the Board of Education? In a *Letter to School Children,* he once had written: "In Massachusetts there are 200,000 children of whom I have the care. I never lie down to sleep nor rise from it, without thinking of them." Could he desert them now?

Perhaps it was Mary who helped her husband see that the reforms he had begun could go on under other leadership. The Board of Education had acquired a permanent place in the state and would continue to consolidate the common schools. The normal schools would carry on their successful work of making teaching a profession. The ten-day institutes to keep teachers in touch with new developments had certainly been popular enough to go on. Improved courses and textbooks were showing excellent results. The additional number of schools would surely attract more pupils. As for the children, could not this new position give the secretary a wonderful opportunity to promote better public education for all children in all the states and territories in the United States?

In Washington he might work to establish a national department of public education. And certainly with a family to support and debts to pay off, he needed the higher salary that the new office would bring. So, despite his misgivings, Horace Mann agreed to serve a new cause.

He began his duties in Washington in mid-April; two weeks later his third son was born. But it was many months before the congressman had a chance to see the little newcomer. Almost immediately he found himself involved in the slavery issue. He made his position clear without hesitation. He opposed oppression of any kind and enslavement most of all, but, like Socrates, he believed that changes should be made by passing new laws, not by breaking those that exist.

Horace Mann knew that congressmen representing the slaveholders had long been a powerful group in the legislature. So he was surprised when, despite his vigorous opposition to their proposals, he was elected to the House of Representatives after the term he was filling expired. His activities in behalf of abolition and his controversy with Daniel Webster advanced the civil rights movement even then. He believed that slavery should be barred from those vast territories that had not yet become states in the Union. He would have none of Webster's stormy plea for compromise.

Horace Mann never wavered from his convictions. "I know one thing," he said. "If I stand by the principles of truth and duty, nothing can inflict on me any permanent harm." His courage in speaking out impressed even his bitterest enemies. Leaders in the state who believed that the Territories had to be "free soil" saw in him their most effective champion. They chose the fearless congressman as their candi-

date for governor of Massachusetts. Again he fulfilled his obligation to society. He ran for the gov-
ernorship, but lost the election.

In the spring of 1852, Horace Mann was offered the presidency of a new college. In Yellow
Springs, Ohio, they had begun to build coeducational Antioch College. Here both sexes were to be
educated equally without racial or religious distinction. Here the buildings and equipment would be
new and up-to-date. Here the president would have
a free hand with the educational program. A salary
of three thousand dollars a year and a fine new home
for his family were assured him. He accepted the
position.

Horace Mann was accustomed to facing seemingly insurmountable problems, and the new position promised more than he had ever experienced.
The college that had been described so glowingly
had to be "approached through mud up to the an-
kles." Not one of the buildings had been completed,
and the president's home was still in the planning
stage. No one had thought to provide temporary
quarters for him. Happily, a large boardinghouse,
whose summer residents had left, was opened to
him and his teachers, and they settled there.

With his customary confidence, the new president ignored the deplorable conditions. This would
be a pioneer experiment and would eventually bring
compensations for present discomforts, he assured
his teachers. With equal faith, he moved his family

from their pleasant home in West Newton to Yellow
Springs, Ohio, in time to witness his inauguration on
October 2, 1853.

Head held high, keen eyes alight with fervor,
Horace Mann was an impressive figure as he stood
erect, self-assured, and enthusiastic before an audience of three thousand. When the new president
ended his acceptance speech, he knew that he had
won their approval. If he had any doubts about the
future of Antioch, he refused to acknowledge them.
He had promised to set high standards for the college, and perhaps he made the entrance examinations too difficult for people of varying ages, back-
grounds, and schooling. Out of 158 applicants, only
eight passed. The others had to enter preparatory
classes.

The students took the physical hardships in their
stride. When on rainy days they had to slosh between buildings in puddles over their shoetops,
when they had to walk a quarter of a mile for clean
water, when they had to huddle in their coats because the stoves had not arrived, and when pigs
wandered through the doorless halls into the dining
room, they offered little complaint. The college,
with its inspiring president, interested teachers, and
new methods, more than made up for most of the
inconveniences.

The problems of securing good teachers, taking
care of the students' needs, and getting the buildings into livable condition were serious enough for
Horace Mann. It was fortunate that he did not know

then that the college was on the verge of bankruptcy from the beginning. His salary of three thousand dollars a year became two thousand, then fifteen hundred, with no assurance of when it would be paid. He had to spend his vacations lecturing in order to take care of his own financial obligations. But eventually the Mann family moved into the promised house, managed somehow to meet their personal expenses, and found pleasure in the progress of the students during those beginning years of Antioch. At the first commencement sixteen, among them three women, were graduated.

During his secretaryship, Horace Mann had become known as an authority on education. Now the story of his achievements in Yellow Springs was spreading. He began to receive offers of positions in other colleges. His family and friends, realizing the increasing pressures at Antioch, urged him to make a change. They saw the hard-working educator martyring himself for a hopeless cause; but he would not believe it.

Although much of his reduced salary was still unpaid, Horace Mann was selling his personal holdings to help pay Antioch's debts, refusing to admit that he was dropping his contributions into a bottomless pit. Even after the college property had been sold at auction, the president clung to his "faith in the improvability of man" — and the improvability of the bankrupt institution through public-spirited people. He was like a farmer with a plow who has struck a rock and will not give in until he has moved it. Finally his faith and devotion encouraged friends to continue financial support for the college. Antioch was reorganized and began to show promise of stability.

President Mann's baccalaureate address of 1859 remains a light to guide all future students. Looking into the intent, expectant faces as he spoke, his words reached out to touch each listener personally. He recounted some of the advances that he himself had worked for. He pointed out that there would always be evils in the world crying for correction. He urged the young men and women about to enter their careers to go forth and give of themselves for the common welfare. And when he concluded with his stirring plea: "Be ashamed to die until you have won some victory for humanity," there was a breath-catching pause before the ripple of approval filled the chapel.

President Mann never realized his own victory, for he became ill the next day. Despite his exhaustion and physical suffering, he fulfilled his scheduled duties for the next forty-eight hours. Then he took to his bed. His wife and children, who had also developed the same undiagnosed, lingering ailment eventually recovered. But the husband, father, teacher and crusader, deprived of the strength he had poured into his work, could not break the hold of this new opponent, this strange illness. At last he was told that he had only a few hours to live. Then, like Socrates, the teacher of a nation spoke to his disciples — those students who were still in Yellow

Springs. He touched the hand of each — and left him a legacy of ideals to live by. Still an educator, he shared his last moments with his pupils while his wife Mary sat beside him — and understood.

More than a century has passed since Horace Mann spoke those words of advice, yet his name is a household word to thousands of children who study each weekday in school buildings named after him. To many times that number he is known as the "Father of American Public Education." Our respected public schools, with their trained teachers, graded classes, improved courses of study and modern equipment, free textbooks, lengthened school year, and freedom from fear of cruel corporal punishment, all are part of the American reformer's dream come true. "In him the citizen, prophet, and schoolmaster are united," wrote French educator Felix Pécaut. Those words proved prophetic, for today the interest of the whole civilized world in education is a continuing tribute to Horace Mann's belief that "the common school is the greatest discovery ever made by man." Today public school education has become the passport from poverty and many other ills to freedom and progress.

IX

THREE WOMEN
LAUNCH AN ERA IN EDUCATION

"Most of you will probably live to be one hundred," prophesied Miss Rosemary Park, president of Barnard College, to the young women about to enter college in 1963. "If you want to keep from being a stuffy old bore for forty years, that is between sixty and one hundred, you've got to learn to be something now. . . . To be young and feminine at sixteen is no achievement. . . . To be a respected person at sixty is."

Bright ambitious high school girls may not be able to picture themselves at that advanced age, but most of them are certain that they will achieve this goal. They accept Eleanor Roosevelt's prediction that "in the years ahead many of the barriers to women's aspirations will disappear." They see women pushing aside one barrier after another by proving themselves in jobs ranging from train conductors, policewomen, and assembly-line workers to doctors, lawyers, and engineers. They know that women have already distinguished themselves in politics, a few in the United States Senate and House of Representatives, more than two hundred in state legislatures, and a half dozen as ambassadors to foreign countries.

"The weaker sex! Who says so?" scoff the modern misses. "Senator Margaret Chase Smith was a candidate for President. Some day a woman will win."

Yet less than a century and a half ago a woman's place was strictly in the home. Even schooling beyond the three R's was not for her.

"If women become scholars, who's to make the puddings and pies?" was a common retort to those who protested.

"Young ladies are not capable of learning men's subjects," some insisted.

"Women are too frail. They cannot stand the strain of advanced education," others objected.

Fortunately, even during Horace Mann's time, a few young ladies who were discerning enough to resent the waste of women's talents were daring enough to do something about it. Emma Hart Willard was one of the pioneers.

Emma Willard

The sprawling farmhouse in Berlin, Connecticut, that welcomed this new child in 1787 certainly needed to be large, for Emma was next to the youngest of seventeen children. Her father, Captain Samuel Hart, was a respected farmer and conscientious citizen. Her mother was as devoted to her seven stepchildren as to her own brood of ten. The interest and affection of both parents kept the overflowing household happily working, studying, and planning ahead.

Like young Horace Mann, the Hart children attended the local district school. They sat for hours on hard, backless benches, each waiting a turn to step over the bench and recite the lesson. They were glad for this meager schooling, but their broader learning came during the long winter evenings at home.

As soon as the chores were done, they gathered around the blazing fire with their parents to talk over schoolwork, farm problems, and local politics — or to listen fascinated while their father or mother read to them from the few treasured books at hand. Emma, especially, drank in knowledge.

When an academy opened not far from her home, she begged permission to use part of a small legacy for the tuition. Two years in this school rounded out her education. Then, at the age of seventeen, she gladly agreed to teach for the summer in a one-room district school in the Kensington section of Berlin.

Her first hours as schoolmistress showed the surprised girl that taking full charge of a classroom was more than doling out book-learning. Her pupils of varying ages, sizes, and abilities looked her over and decided that this fair-haired, blue-eyed teacher was young, inexperienced, and easy. They ignored her directions, chattered loudly to each other, wandered about the room, and even played outside during school hours. Helplessly Miss Emma waited until the end of the morning session. Then she went directly to the woman who had urged her to take charge of the school. With cheeks blazing, she poured out her troubles.

The woman had her own ideas of discipline. That afternoon she sent her young son to school with "a bundle of rods" as a hint to the teacher.

Work on the farm had given Emma a strong right arm. Within the hour she used it, hesitantly at first but more vigorously as the afternoon wore on. Thereafter she had no need for the rods.

The summer flew. By the time the school session ended, Emma felt sure that she would continue to teach. But now she herself yearned to go on studying. Fortunately, her brothers could afford to pay her tuition for two terms at private schools in Hartford. During the summers she earned small fees by teaching children in a classroom that she set up in the family farmhouse. Then when her own studies ended, she accepted a position in the academy in Berlin, her hometown.

Miss Emma was a good teacher. She knew how to keep order and she had a knack for making her pupils study their lessons willingly. News of her excellent work spread beyond Connecticut; and she was offered teaching positions in three states. She accepted the one in Westfield, Massachusetts, but soon moved on to Middlebury, Vermont. There she was given complete charge of Middlebury Female Academy.

Confident and successful, Miss Emma enjoyed her work. Her students appreciated and loved their teacher. But a competitor for the attention of the attractive, energetic young woman lived in Middlebury. In 1809 Emma Hart married Dr. John Willard, a prosperous widower who had given up his medical practice to serve as marshal of the state of Vermont. The twenty-two-year-old bride had so much in common with her fifty-year-old husband that she never felt the difference in their ages.

With three stepchildren at home and a small son born a year later, Emma Willard had little time to think of educating other people's children. But she could no more give up studying than give up eating. She dipped into her husband's medical library and found physiology and the other sciences as fascinating as history, geography, and literature. If ever she taught again, she told herself, she would introduce her pupils to these new wonders of learning.

She faced this prospect much sooner than she anticipated. Business and political reverses brought a change in her husband's fortunes. He lost his position with the state and had to mortgage his property to pay his debts. Even so, he rebelled when Emma decided to teach again. "A husband should support his wife and family," he argued.

"But I like to teach," Emma insisted. "Certainly I could keep a better school than those around me, and it would be no problem to open a school in our own large home."

Finally Dr. Willard admitted the logic in her reasoning; and, in 1814, the Middlebury Female Seminary opened its doors to students.

Emma Willard had not been boasting. In a short time, the school in her home had attracted seventy students. Living so near to Middlebury College, then a school for young men, the schoolmistress found out its requirements, standards, and the courses offered there. As she compared the advantages in men's higher education with the meager provisions for women, she rebelled at the injustice.

She knew very well that even the equivalent of high school education for girls was almost unheard of in most states. And a college education was considered unthinkable. Yet in her own school she was teaching advanced mathematics, history, and languages, and her pupils mastered these without growing a bit less feminine. She directed many class discussions and saw that girls could talk intelligently on thought-provoking topics.

Why should the education of my sex be limited

in subject matter? she asked herself. Why should
private schools for girls concentrate on embroidery,
music, dancing, and a smattering of French, rather
than on solid subjects like those studied by young
men? And why should even this little be available
only to the rich? The legislature should do something about it.

As these thoughts churned in her mind, Emma
Willard began to work out a plan for improving the
schooling for her sex. But for several years, until she
developed it in every detail, she kept her idea secret
from all but her understanding husband. Finally,
she completed the project.

She had heard that Mr. DeWitt Clinton, governor of New York State, approved of higher education for women. And she was certain that an influential patron of her school — who lived in Waterford,
New York — would present her *Plan for Improving
Female Education* to the governor. She realized that
a plan that asked for "large buildings, a library, a
body of trustees for regulating and supervising the
seminary, and financial aid from the state" might
alarm rather than convince the lawmakers. But at
least it would make them notice her proposals. If she
could secure the governor's attention, his reaction
might tell her how to proceed.

The influential gentleman did intercede for the
intrepid schoolmistress; and the governor was impressed. Later when Mrs. Willard sent copies of the
plan to John Adams and Thomas Jefferson, they
thought well of her recommendations. And when

the governor presented it in an address before the state legislature, the congressmen, too, were interested.

Citizens from Waterford, New York, had already urged Mrs. Willard to establish her school in their town. Now she decided that it might be an ideal place for trying out her plan. She lost no time. In the spring of 1819 she officially opened the Waterford Academy for Young Ladies. But the ambitious schoolmistress ventured too soon. Although the legislature had granted the necessary charter and the Senate approved an appropriation of two thousand dollars, the House of Representatives voted against alloting the money. After two years of hoping for state assistance, this rejection was a severe blow.

During this time, other towns were envying Waterford its dynamic crusader for better education for women. When the news of her failure to secure the necessary funds reached Troy, New York, citizens there came forward with a tempting offer.

"We will provide a suitable building and grounds and money enough to get a school under way, if you will set up a seminary in Troy," said their representative.

Without financial assistance from somewhere Emma Willard could not have carried on the growing academy in Waterford much longer. So the determined educator moved to Troy, this time into a three-story building on enough ground for others to be erected when needed. Almost immediately, Troy Female Seminary, with its curriculum of solid subjects, became a model for other schools for women.

Dr. Willard did not stand by idly. His combination of medical training and business experience made him an ideal partner in the venture. As doctor and business manager for the seminary, he handled a heavy share of the work.

Increasingly Emma Willard saw the influence that a teacher could have on her students. Yet she realized how few stimulating teachers were available, especially for girls' schools. Troy Female Seminary, therefore, had a duty to train girls for this career. But what about the capable girls who could not afford this education? Many would make excellent teachers, she knew. So Mrs. Willard worked out another plan. For promising young women interested in teaching, her school would provide tuition, lodging, and clothing if necessary, and wait for payment until the graduates were earning a salary. Thus she offered one of the earliest student-loan programs.

One goal was uppermost, however. Troy Female Seminary must assure every one of its students a thorough academic background. To the usual fashionable subjects Emma Willard added algebra, geometry, geography, and science. In order to be sure of her scientific facts, she studied privately under a professor who lectured on the subject in Troy. She ignored the critics who were appalled at the nonsense of such education for women.

Still another problem could not be easily shrugged off. Few textbooks were available for girls' schools, and most of these the principal considered entirely unsatisfactory for her seminary. There was only one solution. She would have to write others herself. For the first, she collaborated with another author on the *Woodbridge and Willard Geography*, which was published in 1823. By herself, she wrote *Republic of America* and *Willard's Universal History*. When the books came out, the author was surprised at the praise they received from other educators. With growing enthusiasm, she continued to write books to the end of her life.

In a short time Troy Female Seminary became noted for its excellent students. Private schools in many parts of the country wrote asking for teachers trained under Mrs. Willard's supervision. The entire state of New York was proud of this progressive institution. Many came to observe in the school. When General Lafayette toured the United States, he accepted the principal's invitation to visit the seminary; and the girls outdid themselves in honoring the French statesman.

He was so delighted with their festivities for his benefit and so impressed with the school that he stopped there again on his return trip some months later. Before he left, he promised Mrs. Willard a hearty welcome whenever she could find time for a trip to France.

Through all these years, Dr. Willard had been his wife's able assistant. They had worked together in complete harmony and understanding. His expert handling of the school's finances had relieved her of a great burden. His wise counsel helped crystallize many of her decisions. His companionship and pleasure in her successes increased her sense of security. When he died in 1825, Emma felt as though a strong prop had suddenly been withdrawn. Yet even in her grief, the widow's thoughts turned to her school.

She went on teaching, supervising, planning, experimenting, and searching for better methods of instruction. Honors continued to come her way. Governor Clinton took ever greater pride in this woman who had made advanced education possible for so many capable young ladies. Within the next few years, the seminary was enlarged twice, new ground was purchased, and new buildings were erected.

Finally in 1830 Mrs. Willard felt free to leave her school in the care of her widowed youngest sister, Almira Lincoln, who for some years had been her efficient vice-principal. She wanted to see for herself how other countries were educating their girls. Perhaps she could bring back some ideas that were better than her own. But no self-respecting woman of her time could travel very far alone without risking gossip. So her son John accompanied her.

While in Paris, Mrs. Willard wrote to her sister: "From General Lafayette and his delightful family, I have met a reception beyond deserts and expectations." She was given tickets to the House of Deputies and to the theater, was invited to numerous parties, and was presented to Louis Philippe's queen. But her visits to the schools of Paris, London, and

Glasgow, which were to have been the high spots of her trip, proved disappointing.

After seven months in Europe, the traveler returned to Troy refreshed and invigorated. She took up her duties eagerly. The school enrollment had grown to one hundred boarding students and two hundred day students — and was running so well that Mrs. Willard no longer needed to teach. She could spend her time guiding the teachers and students and improving the course of studies. Many new schools patterned after the Troy seminary had already sprung up throughout the country, but important people still chose Mrs. Willard's school for their daughters. And whenever the seminary held its public examinations, heads of colleges, legislators, ministers, school administrators, and parents attended. Always they were impressed by the girls' ability to master "men's" subjects.

By 1837 Emma Willard's published books had made her a wealthy woman. Even so, she considered it a major victory when the New York State Legislature granted Troy Female Seminary "an allotment from the State Literary Fund." This was not the endowment she had so persistently asked for, but it was a substantial sign of recognition of her aims.

By this time John Willard was graduated from West Point and had married a Troy Seminary graduate who was teaching there. So Mrs. Willard turned over the school to her son and his wife. Then she accepted a proposal of marriage. Still a handsome, vivacious, charming woman, she had been wooed and won by a widower, Dr. Christopher Yates of Albany. After their marriage, they went to Boston to live; and almost immediately the bride realized that she had made a grave mistake.

Her second husband's extravagances drained her resources from the start. Still worse, he scoffed at her daily religious devotions and her other ideals. For a time the saddened woman hoped that he would change, but when her health began to break under the strain, she left Dr. Yates and returned to Berlin, where an older sister lived.

She had no intention of ever resuming her teaching, until she met Henry Barnard. Like Horace Mann, the Connecticut educator was touring his state, pointing out the sad conditions in the common schools and urging better teachers for Connecticut's children. He knew about Emma Willard's tireless efforts to make broader education available to girls. So when he was scheduled to speak in the Kensington section of Berlin, Dr. Barnard asked her to write an address for the meeting.

She went to work eagerly and wrote a moving account of more than six thousand Connecticut children who did not attend school at all and of the inferior public schooling of the others. Her suggestions so impressed the listeners that before long she was elected superintendent of the schools in the area.

Improvement of the common schools of Connecticut now became her project. Not only did she instruct children herself, but she held classes and gave demonstration lessons for teachers. Recognizing the importance of interesting mothers in the education of their children, she organized in Kensington "The Female Common School Association." Emma Willard was pursuing her mission again, campaigning strenuously for teacher-training.

Four years of success in this new venture and legal freedom from Dr. Yates gave her enough confidence to return to Troy — no longer as principal of the seminary but as a proud observer of the successful school, a cordial hostess, and a wise counselor to the teachers and students who visited her in her own small brick house near the seminary.

People still refused to let Mrs. Willard retire. In 1845, her written address on the importance of trained teachers was read at the County Superintendents' Convention in Syracuse. Her recommendations so inspired the educators that they persuaded her to carry her message and methods to teacher institutes in other counties of New York State.

With a former student as a companion, Emma Willard set out in her carriage and traveled seven hundred miles, stopping in town after town to instruct teachers and speak to groups of women. The response to her tour was so enthusiastic that the following year she "journeyed eight thousand miles through the West and South by stage coach, packet, and canal boat," appealing to women to do their share in raising the educational standards of the common schools.

In addition, Emma Willard was still writing

books, articles, and speeches, all concerned with education. In 1854, she went to Europe again, this time to represent women at the World's Educational Conference in London. On this trip, too, the American educator thoughtfully measured foreign schools and found them wanting. But she rejoiced in the convention because of the stimulus it would give to educators all over the world.

Her own country was deep in the controversy over the slavery issue; and Emma Willard stood on the side of compromise. She had no strong convictions on slavery, yet she felt that a break in the Union would make the situation worse. But war did come; and, in 1864, the aging educator wrote her *Plan for Universal Peace*. Far ahead of her time, she recommended that the nations of the world form a permanent tribunal to which they would refer their disputes.

Some years later she moved into the seminary to be near her son and his family. But she remained as independent as ever. Distinguished visitors and friends still sought her out. And Mrs. Willard, "in a trailing gown of black velvet or satin, set off by the rich, creamy laces of her head-dress, neck-ruff, and hand-ruffles" gave them a regal but cordial welcome.

She exulted in the advanced subjects taught in the new female seminaries — Mount Holyoke, Vassar, Elmira, and in Oberlin and Antioch, the daring coeducational schools of higher learning. She was justly proud when people told her that these had been inspired by her own undaunted stand for equality of education for the sexes. Busy to the last, the gallant pioneer died in 1870 at the age of eighty-three. Troy Female Seminary, later renamed the Emma Willard School, remains a living monument to its founder, an inspiration to teachers throughout the country, and a symbol of the hard-won freedom for women.

Catharine Beecher

Another crusader who dared to defy the tradition of reserving higher education for men was Catharine Esther Beecher. She was born at the turn of the nineteenth century, the first child of Roxana and Lyman Beecher, a minister in East Hampton, Long Island.

Catharine could always recapture the sense of adventure that seized the whole family when in 1810 they moved from that drab village to Litchfield, Connecticut, where her father had accepted a call to serve in the Congregational Church. What a change it was for the children, now numbering five, to live in a fairyland setting of hills and lakes, trees and flowers. What a pleasure it was for their parents to live in a town that boasted the first law school in the country and a well-known seminary for young ladies. How wonderful it was for the whole family to live in a two-story farmhouse roomy enough to welcome the new people who came to spend hours talking with Dr. Beecher. And how much fun it was to hear their gentle mother — who was almost shy in company — out-argue their brilliant father on the same topics, after the men had gone. It was here, no doubt, that the seeds for later liberal ideas found a waiting place in playful young Catharine's thoughts.

The child's earliest education had been under the watchful eye of her mother, who taught her the three R's and also to sew, knit, draw, and paint. But she responded most enthusiastically to her Aunt Mary's interest in literature, which helped to guide her creative mind. She found housework as dull as arithmetic, but here her mother was adamant. Any girl of hers had to know how to perform household duties. Later Catharine gave her mother the credit for her own disciplined habits. In her *Reminiscences,* she wrote: "It was my good fortune to be born in humble circumstances, the eldest of thirteen children . . . most of them under my care through infancy and childhood." But always she spoke of her father as a playmate in her youth and adviser throughout her life.

Dr. Beecher could not afford to send his daughters to private schools. But Miss Sarah Pierce, who ran the girls' seminary in town, often came to him for advice. In return she accepted his girls without charge. Catharine entered her school when she was ten years old.

Sitting on the long plank bench behind a pine desk, she listened avidly to Miss Pierce read and quote poetry. For the rest, the teacher let her "slide by easily, complaining only that the minister's

daughter was the busiest of all creatures doing nothing."

Before long, the old farmhouse began to grow
cramped, even after a new wing was built. Although
Dr. Beecher's salary was double what he had earned
in East Hampton, the family had increased. So his
wife added to their income by taking in boarders
from Miss Pierce's school. The minister's brilliant
sermons and increasing influence brought more visitors daily; and the children listened fascinated to
the intellectual discussions at home. Despite their
struggle to make ends meet, the family radiated
happiness. Then tragedy stilled their gaiety.

When she was thirteen years old Catharine lost
her beloved Aunt Mary and faced her first great
grief. Three years later, Roxana Beecher died of the
same wasting disease, tuberculosis, leaving her eight
children motherless. Now Catharine was too busy
for mourning. Although her father's stepmother and
sister moved into the parsonage to care for the
motherless household, they could not restore the
pleasant life created by Roxana Beecher.

It was a relief, therefore, when Dr. Beecher married Miss Harriet Porter of Portland, Maine, and
brought home that "beautiful lady with bright blue
eyes and soft auburn hair" who greeted the children
lovingly and won their hearts at once.

Quiet, refined, orderly Harriet Porter Beecher
became an ideal stepmother. She set the house in
perfect order and kept the children in line "without
needing to scold." When she wrote to her family, she

said of her oldest stepdaughter: "Catharine is a fine-looking girl, and in her mind I find all that I expected." Catharine, in turn, accepted her stepmother's standards and soon was busy taking care of Harriet's children as they came along.

When she was nineteen years old, Catharine decided that she ought to earn her own living and relieve her parents of some expense. Since the only occupation open to young ladies of her social class was teaching, she set about to prepare herself in the subjects she would need. Now she studied diligently and surprised herself by her enthusiasm for learning. In a year and a half she had mastered her required subjects and secured a position teaching in New London, Connecticut.

The young woman had never outgrown the interest in writing inspired by her revered Aunt Mary. She still read poetry eagerly and wrote verse from time to time. Some of her poems, signed C.D.D., had been published in the *Christian Spectator* and caught the attention of a brilliant young professor at Yale College, who himself wrote verse as well as textbooks. Here was a person he wanted to meet; and he soon found a friend who could introduce them. From the very first, Alexander Metcalf Fisher felt entirely at home with Miss Catharine and the teeming family. Before long he had Dr. Beecher's permission to "pay his addresses" to his daughter; and a steady exchange of letters kept them in touch with each other between the professor's rare visits.

In the girls' school in New London Catharine

taught successfully, but during the second year, she made up her mind to study the "higher branches" — algebra, geometry, and chemistry. With this background, she would be ready for an independent career. Meanwhile, Professor Fisher was making plans for self-improvement, too. He had decided that a trip to Europe would broaden his education. Before he left, however, he proposed to Catharine who promised to marry him as soon as he returned home.

Then she went on with her work, content to wait for his return. That happy time never came. Two months after the young man sailed on the *Albion*, sad news reached the Beechers. During a severe storm the ship had gone down near the coast of Ireland.

Bewildered and heartsick, Catharine searched her mind and her religion, but could not accept this cruel fate — not so much for herself as for her brilliant fiancé. For months she grieved. Then gradually her sorrow lifted. As she began to find peace and understanding, she decided that there was one thing she could do. She could spend the rest of her life helping others. Immediately, she began to make plans.

Since her vocation was teaching, she would dedicate herself to improving the lot of women through education. Her brother Edward was head of a boys' school in Hartford, Connecticut. Why not organize a seminary for girls in the same town? As usual, Catharine acted promptly. As soon as she learned that influential citizens in Hartford wanted the

school, she began to look for suitable quarters and
finally located a room over a harness store. There, in
the spring of 1823, she and her sister opened the
Hartford Female Seminary for girls "twelve years
old and over."

Since a private school was often judged by the
number of subjects it offered, Miss Catharine added
courses until she was teaching logic, rhetoric, chemistry, Latin, and moral philosophy, while her sister
heard the left-over recitations. The pupils had no
idea how hard their schoolmistress had to work to
keep up with her classes. Fortunately, Edward
Beecher willingly tutored his sister, especially in
Latin, in which she managed to keep just a few days
ahead of the class. Yet she must have done very well,
for the seminary grew so popular that twice the two
teachers had to look for larger quarters.

Their second schoolroom, in the basement of a
church, hummed with the activities of nearly one
hundred students. What a task they had trying to
keep order! The difference in the abilities and back-
grounds of their students and the numerous subjects
to be taught required so many different groups that
class periods had to be cut to eight or ten minutes
each. At times the confusion was so great that Catharine felt they were accomplishing nothing.

The determined young woman tried one plan
after another, always seeking greater efficiency. Still
the situation was intolerable. For four years she
worked in vain to bring the seminary up to her
standards. Then she decided that if the townspeople

wanted her school, they had to help her correct the unbearable conditions. She wrote out her aims and what was needed to accomplish them, then bravely presented her request to leading gentlemen of Hartford.

Instead of the enthusiasm she had hoped for, the schoolmistress found that she had shocked most of those gentlemen. How could she expect them to furnish her with a new building, a study hall large enough to seat one hundred girls, a lecture room, six recitation rooms, and a library! The idea was absurd.

But Catharine did not give up easily. If the men would not listen, perhaps the women would. And they did. She secured all that she had asked for, including eight teachers. Many years later, she wrote: "This was my first experience with the moral power and judgment of women."

With renewed inspiration and zest, she went on setting ever higher standards and experimenting with new ideas in her school. Believing that one aim of any program should be the improved health of the pupils, she introduced a course in calisthenics. Agreeing with the general public that homemaking should be the basis for any woman's accomplishments, she included a class in domestic economy. These were the forerunners of courses in physical education and home economics in the curriculums of most schools today. But she emphasized the traditional higher subjects.

The improvements brought more responsibilities

for Catharine Beecher. She had to train and supervise the added teachers, reorganize the curriculum and the classes, revise textbooks to meet her requirements, and manage the many new business problems of the seminary. Her health began to suffer under the strain, and she had to give up her principalship, at least temporarily.

So, after eight years of intensive work, Catharine Beecher left Hartford Female Seminary in the care of the teachers she had trained and joined her father, who had accepted a call to serve as president and professor of theology at Lane Seminary in Cincinnati, Ohio. Here she hoped to regain good health and then possibly return to Hartford. But as soon as she arrived, she was besieged by the residents to establish a seminary in Cincinnati. It was useless to explain that she had come there for a rest. Besides, when she realized how much it was needed, she really wanted to secure teachers and get a school for young ladies under way. But she promised no more.

Miss Beecher could not be content with a halfway job. Here might be her chance to develop a *higher* school for young women, with a faculty and program organized like that of a man's college. The educator's weariness gave way to a burst of energy as she worked to establish Western Female Seminary. From her Hartford school she begged teachers. From her experience there, she set up the courses and scheduled classes to meet her standards of higher education for women. The citizens were delighted, the enrollment multiplied, and soon the seminary was overcrowded.

Luckily, Miss Beecher found a building for rent in an excellent section of the city and transferred her school there without difficulty. But during this time, she had learned that the town had a fund reserved for "general education." So, armed with good reasons, she sought out the trustees of the fund and asked them to use part of it for an endowment for the new school. She pointed out that only with financial backing could Western Female Institute, as her school was now known, become a permanent institution of learning.

The trustees listened, saw her logic, and agreed to grant the money if the citizens would provide a suitable building. Since the rented building was for sale, the enthusiastic educator lost no time in rounding up a committee to solicit donations for the purchase. How she worked! By herself she raised five thousand dollars in pledges, but that fell far short of the twenty thousand dollars needed. The committee, so willing in words, found themselves too busy to go into action. The money was not forthcoming. In 1837 the building that housed the Western Female Institute was sold to another purchaser and the first experiment in higher education for the women of the West came to an end.

Disappointed and exhausted, Catharine Beecher decided to travel for her health. No matter where she went, however, her attention turned to education. In many parts of the West she found appalling conditions. In a book published in 1845, she described dilapidated school buildings with "doors unhung, absent window panes, gaping walls, and muddy, moldering floors . . . with cracks so large that children could fall through them." She told of ignorant, vulgar men who were engaged in poorly-paid teaching simply because they could find no other jobs. Equally distressing were the facts that no trained teachers were available and many children did not attend school at all.

As she left the West and journeyed eastward, a new idea stirred her thought. What of the many unmarried women in the East who might be glad to earn a living by teaching? Why could they not be trained, then sent to the West to give those unfortunate children a chance for good schooling? Why could she herself not organize an exchange program through which teachers without schools could find such employment and schools without teachers could secure them? Straightway, Miss Beecher plunged into this project.

When she was asked to prepare an address for a meeting of the National Lyceum, she pleaded with dramatic fervor for the teacherless children. Many who heard the speech were so moved that they offered their help immediately. But in a day when a lady could not speak before a mixed audience without being criticized, she would need to employ a man to take charge of the teacher placement.

Meanwhile, her brother Thomas was her spokesman in the larger cities, while she traveled, wrote, talked, and persuaded, in behalf of her undertaking. Her treatise *Women, Will You Save Your Country?* prompted many hard-working persons to reach into their savings and send contributions. Another, *The Evils Suffered by American Women and American Children*, was even more moving. In it the author told of "over three thousand schools unfit for man or beast, six thousand schools destitute of convenient seats, eight thousand that lacked ventilation," and a shortage of more than five thousand teachers in a number of states. These reports so aroused Governor Slade of Vermont that he volunteered to help in any way possible — an offer that had far-reaching results.

Now Catharine Beecher had to find a man who could handle the work of the teacher-agency. She urged Henry Barnard to take on the position but the Connecticut educator had his own commitments. She wrote to several other well-recommended men, but they were not interested in her "impracticable" scheme. Then she seized upon Governor Slade's offer, but he was still in office; moreover, he was not certain that he wanted to head this risky venture. The persistent woman used every means of persuasion, until the governor finally agreed to begin work on the agency as soon as his term of office was over.

Before the end of 1846, working together, they had outlined plans for a Board of National Popular Education. Miss Beecher's task was to remain in the East to recruit future teachers for the West, give them a month's training in methods of teaching, and brief them on the situations they might face in the Western schools. The former governor traveled in the West, lecturing to audiences, organizing committees of interested citizens to find out which areas needed teachers, and preparing the people there for them. The program provided several newspapers with material for skeptical and humorous articles. When the first thirty-five teachers set out for their schools, one headline read: "Wives for the West." Undaunted, Miss Beecher went on with her teacher-training courses.

Mr. Slade worked as zealously as Miss Beecher, but he lacked her ability to foresee the problems that might harass the teachers in so unfamiliar an environment. Some found the schools assigned to them intolerable or even nonexistent. Some found their lodgings unbearable. One teacher had to share a two-room shack with a family of ten. One broke a leg. Several fell ill, with no one to look after them. A few justified the newspaper's jibe. They married men in the West and left their schools teacherless. Obviously, steps had to be taken to correct the situation.

"We need another paid agent who will escort the teachers to their posts," Miss Beecher insisted. "We also need an emergency fund to tide them over any financial difficulties that might result from their transfer to the West."

Mr. Slade disagreed. Volunteer citizen committees could handle such situations, without this extra expense, he was sure. Catharine Beecher held out obstinately for greater protection for the teachers. Finally, Agent Slade reorganized the Board of National Popular Education without any plan to assist teachers. He went on lecture tours of his own and led many people in the West to see the necessity for a better educational program. But it was Miss Beecher who raised the money to help the teachers in distress and made provisions to care for them.

She realized that the agency was now out of her hands, but she already had another innovation mentally in the making. Why not establish schools for women in central cities of the West and organize them like men's colleges? Why not also establish a normal school in each city to train local young people to teach in their own Western areas? Then there would be no need to transfer teachers long distances.

She realized that this project, too, would require an agent and money to pay his salary. Now, however, she was ready to cover that expense herself with the royalties from her popular book, *Domestic Economy*.

As always, more money had to be raised. In addition to her tours and writing of speeches, the invincible educator in 1852 founded the American Women's Educational Association, the first of its kind in the country. For a quarter of a century it did much to further her enterprises. Within the next years, three schools for women were established in the West — one in Milwaukee, Wisconsin; another in Dubuque, Iowa; a third in Quincy, Illinois. Each began glowing with promise, but as Miss Beecher constantly pointed out, schools could not survive on tuition fees alone. Without endowments their futures would be uncertain. The years ahead proved her right. Only one continued — Milwaukee-Downer College, which in 1964 merged with Lawrence College to become Lawrence University, in Appleton, Wisconsin.

Catharine Beecher spent the last years of her life in her brother's home in Elmira, New York. At the age of seventy-seven she lectured at Elmira College, established twenty years earlier by others interested in college education for women. She wrote and planned for her great cause until just before her death in 1878.

In more than a half-century of continuous striving for equal opportunities for her sex, Catharine Beecher had seen her country go through many changes and several crises. Wars, financial panics, and the end of slavery had left their trail of unsolved problems. Woman suffrage had already become an issue. She was firmly convinced that the solution could be found in better education for all people, regardless of class, race, or sex.

In a day when other outstanding American educators kept close to their home grounds to test and develop their projects, Catharine Beecher launched her revolutionary crusade in then-distant parts of the country and persisted doggedly until she set the wheels rolling toward her goal. When speeches failed to bring results, she put her ideas into print — in circulars, pamphlets, and books. At a time when good teachers were few because the work was derided, underpaid, and unattractive, she took steps to make teaching a profession. In an era when, except for the impoverished who had to earn a living as servants or factory workers, women had few vocations, Catharine Beecher saw in teaching an ideal career for her sex. She foresaw that freedom for women to secure a solid education could double the rate of progress in her nation.

Mary Lyon

Despite the inferior schooling available to most children and the poor reputation of teaching as a vocation during the early nineteenth century, there were civic-minded persons who taught as a service to their communities. One such was the deacon who served as schoolmaster in the East District School of Buckland, Massachusetts.

As he stood in the doorway of the dingy, one-room building watching his pupils scatter homeward, his eyes followed a sturdy girl whose unruly hair shone like copper in the afternoon sunshine. With the book he had loaned her clutched tightly under one arm, and her body swaying in time to her quick steps, she sped toward a farm nearly two miles away. What a scholar! Imagine a girl wanting to learn grammar! "I wonder what she would make of it if she could attend college," he murmured.

College! Even if colleges had been open to women at that time, the girl, Mary Lyon, could hardly have aspired to one, for like the average young New Englander, Mary was growing up the hard way. She was born in 1797, the fifth living child of Jemima and Aaron Lyon, whose small hillside farm, rocky and arid under its summer trimming of colorful wild flowers, produced just enough to feed and clothe the family. The arrival of two more girl-babies in the next few years made the struggle greater. Yet they were a happy, hopeful household until Aaron Lyon died, leaving his wife to shoulder the responsibilities of the farm and seven children.

Luckily, Widow Lyon had a strong constitution and complete faith in a benevolent Providence. The six girls helped with the home chores, spinning, weaving, and sewing; their brother did his share of the outdoor work; and they attended the nearest district schools during their sessions.

When Mary was thirteen years old, her mother remarried and took her two youngest daughters to her new husband's home in nearby Ashfield. The three older girls had already married; so Mary kept house for her brother, who paid her a dollar a week for her uncomplaining help. Carefully she hoarded her earnings, thinking of them as a school fund. After her brother married, although she still lived in the farmhouse and helped care for his children, Mary felt free to look elsewhere for work.

"You should teach," the deacon advised. "I know of a school that needs a teacher for the summer."

So Mary Lyon accepted a position in Shelburne Falls. Here her salary was seventy-five cents a week and "boarding round" — free room and meals in the homes of the children she taught. Indeed, the mothers were delighted when it came their turn to keep the teacher, for she lent a willing hand to any household tasks. To Mary, however, this first teaching experience was a disappointment. The ambitious seventeen-year-old girl who absorbed knowledge so easily could not keep her class in order.

When the summer session closed, she left with a sigh of relief, certain that she was not cut out for a teacher. Yet she went back for another summer and later taught in other district schools in the area. She also sewed, spun, wove, and did housework to add to her fund for further education.

As soon as Sanderson Academy was established in Ashfield, Mary used her small savings to enroll. The eager student did not notice that her coarse, shapeless homemade dress, with a drawstring at the neck and another at the waist, drew sly glances from the other girls. Even her thick, curly auburn hair, that should have caused envy, was piled so carelessly on top of her head that it added to her disheveled appearance. Very soon, however, her classmates forgot her queer clothes and her countrified

manners and speech. The young woman's bright
blue eyes, ready smile, and boundless energy
thawed aloofness, and her scholarship awed even
the teacher. "That Mary Lyon!" muttered more than
one. "What kind of woman learns a whole Latin
grammar in three days and recites in almost every
class!"

Mary's warm, open personality won the friendship of her deskmate, Amanda White, and a happy
friendship it turned out to be. Squire White was a
trustee of Sanderson Academy. When Mary was
about to leave school because her money had run
out, the squire not only saw to it that she was given
free tuition but he also invited her to live in his
home.

After the session ended, Mary taught another
term in Buckland, took a special course for young
women at Amherst Academy, taught school again,
then returned to Ashfield, where she found Amanda
bubbling with excitement. She was going to Byfield
Academy to study under the Reverend Joseph
Emerson.

Mary hugged the lucky girl, wished her joy in
her new school, then escaped to her room, where
Amanda later found her in tears. The honest young
woman could not hide the reason. She wept because
she herself would never have the opportunity to
study under the wonderful Harvard graduate,
whose excellent teaching was known throughout
New England.

"You must come to Byfield with me," Amanda said at once. "I'll see Father about it."

What the spirited girl said to her father is not known, but he promptly offered Mary a loan.

To Mary the summer of instruction was worth losing what she might have earned working, and worth enduring the criticism of persons who felt that Mary Lyon knew enough to teach their daughters without her chasing about for more learning. Professor Emerson was a dedicated teacher who encouraged his students to think for themselves and to discuss what they learned instead of merely parroting the textbook. Mary began to realize how much more than common-school education her sex needed, if they were to do their share in building a better world. Her intelligence and earnestness impressed her instructor and his assistant, Miss Zilpah Grant.

That fall Mary Lyon went back to Ashfield, this time as the first woman teacher in Sanderson Academy. During the next two winters she introduced Mr. Emerson's methods in her classes and was delighted with the results. During this time, too, Zilpah Grant decided to take over the principalship of the Adams Academy in Londonderry, New Hampshire, and she invited Mary Lyon to join her there for the summer. Mary accepted at once. It would be a privilege to work under this stimulating woman.

In the fall of the same year, 1824, Pastor Clark, one of her early teachers, encouraged Mary Lyon to open a school for young ladies in Buckland. The ambitious teacher undertook the experiment eagerly. She rented the upper floor of a large home for her Select Female School, and enrolled twenty-five girls the first term. The enthusiastic students spread such glowing reports of their progress that within a short time she had to transfer her growing classes to a larger home, where the enrollment increased to nearly one hundred. Miss Mary, who at the age of seventeen had almost closed the doors to a teaching career behind her, was now a successful school principal.

Miss Grant, however, was not so content. She had moved on to organize an academy in Ipswich and took most of her pupils with her. She also persuaded her friend Mary to accept a summer position there.

In her own school Mary Lyon had set the fees as low as possible, aiming only to cover expenses. Miss Grant, however, saw the danger in this kind of financing, and had ideas on how it should be corrected. "Schools like ours are better than none for the immediate present," she explained to Mary. "But what will happen when we are no longer here? Suppose the trustees replace us with teachers who do not understand the need for sound subjects, who know nothing of teaching methods or, still worse, who do not care as long as they are paid. Higher schools for girls must have endowments that free them from becoming merely money-making ventures for those who carry them on."

Gradually Mary Lyon began to think the same

way. But her work at Ipswich filled her days and often her nights, too. Because of its high standards, the academy became so popular that the principal decided to keep the school open ten months a year; and she invited Mary Lyon to become her assistant. Although she was reluctant to leave her own school at Buckland, she decided in favor of Ipswich.

Under these two women, this academy gained increasing recognition and attracted students from many states in the Union. From time to time, however, Mary Lyon surveyed the prospering school and wondered whether it, too, would drop out of existence in other hands. Even in her busiest moments, she would find the uncertainty invading her thoughts, demanding action. Why not establish a new seminary financed by an endowment from the beginning? If Zilpah Grant wanted to try, she herself would carry on at Ipswich. If not, Mary Lyon set her shoulders. She was ready for the task.

So in 1834 she cut her ties with Ipswich Academy and began a campaign for a school for young ladies that would offer "an elevated standard of science, literature, and refinement . . ." and that would be "perpetuated by public endowment."

Mary Lyon was thirty-seven years old. She had spent at least half that time teaching. She well knew the difficulties of this undertaking, but she clung to her belief that "one of the nicest mental operations is to distinguish between the very difficult and what is utterly impossible." She decided to pattern the school of her dreams after the academies in Ipswich, Hartford, and Troy — "with room for continued improvement." One improvement she had in mind was to bring the new seminary within the financial reach of middle-class girls.

Miss Lyon had the same handicap as other female pioneers of her day: she dared not go about making speeches before mixed audiences — not because she feared what she called "empty gentility," but because she was afraid that any criticism of her conduct would prejudice people against her project. So she enlisted influential men to assist her. Luckily, she had already impressed Dr. Edward Hitchcock of Amherst, under whom she had studied science, and Dr. Roswell Hawks, whose daughter had been in her Buckland school. Together they rounded up a committee of other prominent men who met with her and listened to her plans. Yet even her staunchest supporters shook their heads at her preposterous proposals.

What did she want? Merely "a few acres of land, attractively located," a comfortable building that would include "a large seminary hall, recitation rooms, a library, a reading room, a chemical room with apparatus, and a dormitory adequate for eighty girls, each to have a room for herself . . ."

How would she finance this expensive project and make it worth the cost?

By collecting money in pledges or cash from the generous public for the basic running needs, by having the young ladies themselves do the cooking, cleaning, and other domestic work on a cooperative basis, by enlisting teachers so dedicated that they would give their services for a minimum wage, and by securing an endowment that would keep the school living and growing generation after generation.

"Impossible," cried many.

"Ridiculous!" railed a newspaper reporter.

"You would make servants of the poorer girls. . . . The wealthier would refuse to do housework." . . . "Better to keep tuition high for those who can pay and thus cover the expenses of the less fortunate." . . . "And what kind of teachers would you get for a pittance?" . . . ran the comments.

Patiently Mary Lyon explained that this was an experiment in which she would ask no more for herself than she asked for the other teachers. She pointed out that the domestic work would not be for cutting down the expenses of the poorer girls. Instead, like the money contributed by philanthropic citizens, it would be a "gratuitous service" to the school by all the students. Besides, it would give them the domestic training all women needed and would be a period of relaxation from study.

With tact and patience, she set out to win the public to her convictions, not by writing books or speeches but by approaching people personally. Going from house to house, she talked to women in their kitchens and reminded them that their daughters would someday be the first teachers of their own children. For this reason, especially, they needed a good education. She talked to their husbands and explained the practical advantages of higher education for their daughters. Every woman needed a vocation and what could be better than a teaching career?

Money was the first essential, she knew. So morning after morning, in good weather and bad, she was off in a carriage with the college professor, the minister, or another co-worker — or in a stagecoach by herself, discussing her project with anyone nearby. Always she emphasized the need for a school that could depend on a stable fund contributed by the public, like the money given to institutions for young men. With her green velvet moneybag ever at hand, she pictured her ambitions so vividly that she herself collected the first thousand dollars from the women of Ipswich and from her students.

Gradually the fund grew. At one meeting three thousand dollars was donated. No amount was so small that Miss Lyon did not appreciate it and none so large that she did not hope for more.

Long before the necessary funds were raised, the committee began to consider locations for the seminary. Several towns offered sites and volunteered part of the money to get the school started. South Hadley, a lovely village not far from the Connecticut River, had fifteen acres of land available and agreed to raise eight thousand dollars in subscriptions toward building the seminary.

Truly a cultural setting, thought Miss Lyon.

The money will ease the financial pressure, agreed the men on the committee.

As for a name, what loftier name could there be than that of the nearby mountain — Mount Holyoke.

When finally ground was broken for the building, the risk was great, for the twenty thousand dollars considered necessary for this step had not yet been collected. But confident that the money would be on hand when it was needed, Mary Lyon had persuaded her co-workers to get the construction under way. All this time she was like a nomad, covering the countryside and preaching that this new-type seminary, which would reach into the homes of the common people for its students, was worth reaching into their pockets for.

In 1836, when the cornerstone of Mount Holyoke Seminary was finally laid, more than one dignitary standing by muttered his doubts. Not so Mary Lyon. She realized how much still needed to be done before her dream could grow into reality, but her faith remained firm. With a full heart she expressed that faith as she prophesied, "This will be an era in female education."

Meanwhile the building rose slowly, and problems kept pace with its growth. Early in its construction, walls caved in and the work had to be started again. As time for the donors to fulfill their pledges drew near, the financial panic of 1837 crept closer. Many contributors had to ask for more time. Un-

daunted, the crusader continued to solicit further
pledges. She dipped into her own meager funds and
gave what she could. Her determination often inspired individuals to give more than they could spare.

Her account books showed $27,000 contributed
by some 1800 persons in ninety-one towns, in cash
and pledges from six cents to one thousand dollars.

But when she set November 8, 1837, for the
opening day of the school, her most sincere well-
wishers were more skeptical than hopeful. Mary
Lyon herself, in a letter to a friend, wrote: "Antici-
pating the date is like looking down a precipice of
many hundred feet which I must descend."

That date arrived all too soon, but the delivery
of furniture, bedding, and other necessities lagged
way behind schedule. Parents looked in on a hectically busy group. More than one father tethered his
horse, took his daughter and her trunk to her new
quarters, then rolled up his sleeves and began to
help the deacons and trustees who were hard at
work tacking down matting, unloading furniture,
setting up beds, and placing heavy equipment.

Mary Lyon, supervising everything, still managed to be a gracious hostess. She welcomed each
newcomer warmly, directed her to her room, and invited her to come back down to help as soon as possible. They all did, promptly joining the women who
were "washing crockery, stacking cupboards, and
giving out bedding. . . ." Certainly no carefully
prepared speech could have broken the ice and initiated the girls into the cooperative housekeeping

plan more quickly. Nor was there time for them to
worry about their entrance examinations which
went on as scheduled, in temporary quarters, with
"some students seated on the stairs or on a pile of
mattresses in a hallway."

Instead of the eighty girls planned for, one hundred sixteen enrolled during the course of that year.
Yet Mary Lyon, ignoring the warnings from Zilpah
Grant and some of the trustees, set the fee for room,
board, and tuition at only sixty-four dollars. What
was more, she had secured dedicated teachers, none
of whom, including herself, received more than two
hundred dollars for the year's salary.

Mary Lyon had mowed down many obstacles
and had cut a clear trail. She had a school plant that
would soon be worth seventy thousand dollars,
every cent of which was coming from voluntary contributions. She had set up a three-year program patterned largely after Ipswich Academy. She had a
Board of Trustees, legally appointed, who were *giving* their services for the good of the seminary. She
had enrolled a group of responsible girls, most of
them from middle-class families, who could afford
Mount Holyoke's modest fees. Now she had to prove
to the scoffers, the doubters, and her faithful associates that her plan "for the education of women . . .
comparable to that in colleges for young men . . ."
would work.

Mary Lyon was still sturdy, pink-cheeked, bright
eyed, and buoyant. She was so engrossed in her educational activities that her graying hair, even under

her turban, still looked unruly. She had lost none of her ability to convince her pupils of the practical value of high ideals. "Education is to fit one to do good," was her motto. Although she had not planned Mount Holyoke Seminary to be strictly a normal school, she guided her girls toward teaching. In simple, straightforward language, she made them see the difference between schoolmistresses who were "mere teachers" and those who were "educators of children."

Cooperation in hard work became the slogan. And no one worked harder than the principal. She lived with and for her students. She was overseer of the building, admissions officer, textbook critic, landscaping consultant, substitute teacher, adviser to teachers and pupils, and recreation director, as well as active correspondent with other educators who were constantly inquiring about her program of studies and seeking teachers for their schools. She was still the magic spirit that continued to open the purses of an increasing number of donors, so that her seminary might be assured of permanence. But she also found time to plan relaxing activities for the girls.

No wonder the principal saw the first year of her great experiment rushing to a close faster than she could keep up with it. But the day of the public examinations came off with credit to all. Rumor spread that one distinguished speaker who had expected to address a class of "female dilettantes" was so impressed by the young ladies' intelligent responses to thought-provoking questions that he hurriedly rewrote his speech to raise it to the level of the students.

Further proof of Mount Holyoke's success soon poured in. Miss Lyon had to turn away four hundred applicants for the next term, many of whom applied for the following year or for the one after that, if space would not be available until then. Finally, even the most doubtful admitted that the building had to be enlarged. So by the fall of 1842 a new wing was ready for occupation and additional teachers were ready for their classes.

Now that the seminary was moving along in comfortable routine, its creative principal concentrated her energies on raising the standards of the school, broadening the content of the courses, improving instruction, and selecting the best teachers available. Remembering her own limited home background, she strove to develop in Mount Holyoke an environment where girls could absorb culture and social ease.

Mary Lyon was practical enough to realize that "knowledge is only a beginning." She believed that knowledge, to be worthwhile, must be put to work. Her common-sense recommendations, grown out of classroom experience and understanding of young people, are as fundamental to good teaching today as they were in her time.

"Make every lesson interesting," she would tell

her teachers-to-be. "But to be interesting, you must be interested yourself — or seem to be," she would add with one of her sudden flashes of humor.

"Make the dull ones think once a day," she would say. "Make their eyes sparkle once a day."

And carried away by the enthusiasm of their instructor, the students could picture themselves brightening the lives of small dullards until Miss Lyon brought them back to reality with the reminder, "You have not governed a child until you can make him smile under your government."

There were still those who warned against the perils in higher education for women, but their voices were weaker, their arguments flimsier. Widespread praise drove criticism to the background. In twelve years, the principal saw the enrollment of her school more than double and the teaching staff more than triple. She met the usual boarding-school problems with wisdom and composure. Her work was never ending because her interest in humanity was unceasing and her faith in the ability of educated women to help build a better world was limitless.

But her resistance was lower than her spirits. In 1849, one of her students contracted erysipelas, and Mary Lyon, although she was just recuperating from a severe attack of influenza, insisted on helping to care for the patient. The girl died and the principal herself contracted the disease. On March 5, news of Mary Lyon's death went out to the people.

The shocked teachers and grief-stricken students at Mount Holyoke Seminary, the three thousand other pupils whom Mary Lyon had taught during her thirty-five years as an educator, and her many friends and associates mourned the loss of a woman of uncommon vision. The monument that marks her grave on the grounds of Mount Holyoke College and the bronze bust in the American Hall of Fame that honors her achievements are both inscribed with her own inspiring words: "There is nothing in the universe that I fear but that I shall not know all my duty or shall fail to do it."

To those who stood beside her during her last hours, she said, "I should like to come back and watch over this institution, but God will take care of it."

Once again her faith was justified. In 1888 Mount Holyoke Seminary received a charter renaming it Mount Holyoke College for Women, the first institution of its kind. Mary Lyon had followed her own precept to the end. "Have a plan . . . work for some purpose . . . but do not expect to make over the world." Yet by her own selfless devotion to her cause, she did make over the world for the women of our time and, through them, for the men of our time, as well. Today Mount Holyoke College can count more than twenty-five thousand graduates, some of whom, like Frances Perkins, the first woman cabinet member, have blazed new trails for their sex.

X

TURN OF THE CENTURY

Your time-craft has slowed, "ticked" gently forward, and touched down on home ground in your own decade of the twentieth century. You have visited with some of the many pioneering master teachers of the past. Now let us look in on a few more recent American pioneers in education. What of Henry Barnard? Horace Mann urged him to head the Lexington Normal School when Cyrus Peirce had to leave because of ill health. And it was Henry Barnard who prompted Emma Willard to devote her last years to improving teaching in the common schools.

Although he had barely a year of general teaching experience, Henry Barnard certainly lent a strong hand in building for freedom and progress. He was a rich man's son who attended private schools and went to Yale College. But until the age of twelve, he was taught in a district school so wretched that he almost ran away from home. The memory of those early years never faded.

After receiving his law degree and traveling in Europe for two years — concentrating on the educational systems in various countries — he was elected to the Connecticut State Legislature, where he had a chance to make recommendations for the improvement of education in his state. When he became the first secretary of the Connecticut State Commission of Education, he launched his own campaign for better schooling for all children, for trained teachers, and for better textbooks and school buildings.

His educational activities were many and varied. He served as Commissioner of the Rhode Island Public Schools for a time, as president of the University of Wisconsin for several years, and as head of St. John's College, Annapolis, for one year. He wrote articles and books on education, one devoted entirely to Pestalozzi's work, and he edited the *American Journal of Education* for thirty years. When in 1867 he was appointed the first United States Commissioner of Education, his recommendations reached and impressed educators in every state in the Union. But his influence had reached out years earlier and continued to the end of his life in 1900. During his eighty-nine years he made no less than fifteen hundred speeches on education.

Francis Wayland Parker was another crusader for the rights of children. He was born in 1837, the son of a New Hampshire farmer who died young and left his family so poor that Francis was "bound out" to a farmer when he was eight years old. The boy had most of his early education during the brief sessions of the local district school, but he spent his spare hours reading the Bible, old almanacs, and anything else he could find. At thirteen he enrolled himself in an academy and did odd jobs to pay his expenses. Even as a lad he dreamed of being a teacher, and he faced his first class at the age of sixteen.

His teaching in New Hampshire and later in Illinois convinced Parker that his country needed a revolution in education. His army experiences during the Civil War filled him with an ambition to educate young people to work for peace. Although he had been a strict disciplinarian as an officer in the army, he hated regimentation, especially the discipline enforced in the schools. He believed that adjustment to the social life in school was just as important as the learning of subject matter.

When he inherited five thousand dollars from a relative, he used it for travel and study in Europe. Then he returned to the United States, "convinced that there was a better way of teaching." He found the opportunity to "explode his new ideas," when he became superintendent of schools in Quincy, Massachusetts. Here he began his experiment in keeping children happily busy in learning-by-doing and in learning from each other. Let the child find his own aptitudes and stimulate him to build on these aptitudes, was Parker's rule. "Lay the foundation for happiness, character, and good citizenship, and knowledge will follow naturally," was his theory.

When he became head of the Cook County Normal School and then of the education department of the University of Chicago, his ideas spread. Teachers trained under him dropped their formal discipline. Good teachers kept the relaxed workshop method well in hand. The classes of weak teachers were soon in an uproar and completely unmanageable. Critics saw only foolish play in such teaching. Reformers saw purposeful, controlled noise that resulted from enthusiastic, interested children working and learning together. Colonel Parker had stirred up the revolution he advocated. Whether teachers called it progressive education or the modern movement, when his system found its pattern it emancipated American children from school drudgery and opened the way to present-day methods.

This was not the only kind of emancipation that added to "the arch of freedom and progress." Booker T. Washington shaped his own building blocks. When it came to problems, he really had them. Born to slave parents, he was just nine years old when the Civil War ended and not much older when his stepfather put him to work, first in a salt furnace and later in the mines of Malden, West Virginia. Even then his great yearning was for schooling — a strange ambition in an era when few Negroes, young or old, could read or write. But young Booker learned his numbers from those on the salt barrels and his letters from a battered spelling book. A little evening tutoring, grudging permission to attend a small school newly opened for Negro children, and somehow by the time he was sixteen years old he managed to get enough education to apply for admission to Hampton Institute in Virginia.

His entrance examination was a practical one. Booker was handed a broom and told to sweep a classroom floor. Sweep it he did, three times over. And when the assistant principal inspected his work, she not only admitted him to the institute, but she gave him a janitorial job to help pay his expenses. After completing his course, he taught for three years in his old school in Malden, studied further, then became an instructor at Hampton Institute.

When he was twenty-five years old, Booker Washington accepted the principalship of a new normal school for training Negro teachers. He was proud of this honor, but disappointed when he found no building, not even a site reserved for it, in Tuskegee, Alabama. But the young man was already expert in tackling impossible situations. He secured a dilapidated church and a tumbledown shanty for temporary quarters. Within three months he had enrolled more than fifty students, hired a lady teacher, and arranged to buy an abandoned plantation nearby. Here a stable and a henhouse served as the first classrooms. Now, however, Principal Washington saw what needed to be done and had an inspiration about how it could be done. Tuskegee Institute must begin by teaching its students how to earn a living. What better training could they get than in building their own school?

As they cleared the land, grew their own food, made the bricks and equipment for the building, and sold their oversupply in town, the students learned the dignity in labor and the townspeople learned to respect Tuskegee Institute's students. Washington's dream of educating "head, heart, and hand" took root and it blossomed into cultural training, too.

Booker T. Washington proved himself more than a practical educator. He was a powerful speaker, and he used this gift in lectures to carry his crusade to the public. His great vision of emancipating his people from ignorance, so that they could take their part in shaping a greater society, stirred his audiences into contributing to his project. Washington traveled as widely, wrote as meaningfully, and lectured as movingly as Horace Mann and Henry Barnard. He became so well-known that four United States presidents consulted him on matters affecting Negro welfare.

Yet he had his critics, too. Even the N.A.A.C.P., which was organized a few years before he died, considered Washington an appeaser because he did not demand political and social equality for his people. But like other educators, he was influenced by the times in which he lived. He knew when to compromise and when to stand his ground. In our time he might have joined hands with Dr. Martin Luther King in the civil rights movement.

At that time, however, his proudest moments came from seeing Tuskegee Institute grow into a great student-operated estate that taught thirty-eight trades to more than fifteen hundred students. It became a model for hundreds of later vocational and technical schools.

When Booker T. Washington died in 1915, he was eulogized throughout the world. American newspapers called him a "modern Moses" and a "man of the ages." Through his work in education, he had built firmly upon the slowly rising arch of freedom and progress.

With these three educators you crossed into the twentieth century. Pause for a moment with John Dewey, another emancipator of children, one who surely influenced the teachers of your parents and probably some of your present teachers, too. He was born in 1859 in Burlington, Vermont, and lived on a farm until his father opened a grocery store in Burlington. He attended the public schools, where he was only an average pupil, but he did well enough to enter the University of Vermont at the age of fifteen. Here stimulating books and teachers turned his attention toward society, its problems, and the need for correcting them. Here his own scholarly thinking had its roots.

After three years as a high school teacher, he entered newly established Johns Hopkins University and was equally fortunate in his teachers. By the time he had earned his degree for graduate work he was on his way to a career in education and philosophy. He taught in universities — Michigan, Minnesota, Chicago, Columbia. At the University of Chicago, he founded the Laboratory School, an experimental elementary school where he tried out his own ideas of how children should be taught.

Dewey scorned the traditional system of making the children sit quietly in orderly rows, listlessly trying to learn the facts that adults considered important. "Education is growth," he pointed out. "It is not the business of the teacher to prepare children for adult life." They must be educated to live fully and meaningfully at every stage of their development. In John Dewey's philosophy, the child, rather than the subject matter, is the hub about which the school should be centered.

Like Pestalozzi and Froebel, he believed that a good teacher should be able to direct the natural interests of the children so that they would grow mentally and socially as they grew physically. "The school is their social world," he would insist. "It must give them experience in social activities." Dewey urged teachers to give children freedom to question, argue, and express their individuality. Only thus would they develop their own powers and grow into well-adjusted adults.

Older people were horrified. "That man Dewey," they stormed, "is using the children as guinea pigs. He'll be the ruination of public school education."

At Columbia University Teachers College, John Dewey opened the eyes and minds of thousands of teachers to the need for a different attitude toward

the education of young people. His countless articles in periodicals, his numerous scholarly books,
and his thoughtful lectures wherever he traveled
throughout the world caused greater controversy
than Parker's experiments. "Dewey, not Parker, has
fathered this distortion of common-sense teaching,"
his opponents warned. "Take his ideas with a ton of
salt."

But Dewey's followers agreed with him that the
chief difference between work and play is that work
is forced upon one, while play develops from sponta-
neous interest. They agreed that school could be
made fun if teachers permitted the children to move
about, learn with their hands as well as with their
heads, mingle freely with their companions, and
thus live in a normal school society.

With Dewey they believed that in a democracy
the educational systems should also be democratic.
The pupils should have a part in planning class activities and the teachers should participate in decid-
ing school policies — policies that "must be compat-
ible with the times."

"Every teacher," said John Dewey, "should realize the dignity of his calling. . . ." And through all
his recommendations ran the theme that every
teacher must recognize the dignity of the child as
well.

With freedom and encouragement to think, to
question, to disagree, to speak out, to experiment
with new methods, to write controversial books and
articles, the great teachers of the twentieth century

come too fast for a quick survey. As William Van Til points out, "This is a period when people whose names will never be celebrated serve humanity — unsung members of the Peace Corps, teachers at obscure international outposts and still less recognized classrooms off Main Street, U.S.A., scholars stubbornly searching for truth, citizens defending free inquiry . . ."

Yes, in unison with the Greats of the past and the present, the unsung teachers are building the arch that leads to freedom and progress. They are proving General Omar Bradley's thesis that "the teacher is the real soldier of democracy; others can defend it, but only he can make it work." They are reaching for the utopia where the arch can be joined by the keystone, that final block which is still being shaped of the Socratic ideals — wisdom, courage, temperance, and justice — in which all others may be found.

Striving with them are millions of dedicated persons who know that they can only approach the perfect society, never reach it. For "the story of education is the story of mankind." As such it is never ending.

FOR FURTHER READING

The early sources used for information on *Freedom Builders* are not only too numerous to include here but most of them would be unavailable to readers who do not have access to large libraries. Those who wish to study the various personalities in depth may find some of these sources listed in the acknowledgments which follow this selected bibliography. The publications below will add to the pictures of the pioneer-teachers. Titles marked with an asterisk are published in paperback.

Chapters 1, 2, 3

Aristotle. *On Man in the Universe: Metaphysics. Parts of Animals. Ethics. Politics. Poetics.* Edited with introduction by Louise Ropes Loomis. New York: Walter J. Black, 1943.

Davis, William Stearns. *A Day in Old Athens.* Boston: Allyn & Bacon, 1914.

*Hamilton, Edith. *The Greek Way to Western Civilization.* New York: New American Library, 1961.

Levy, Gertrude R. *Plato in Sicily.* London: Faber & Faber, 1956.

Plato. *Apology. Crito. Phaedo. Symposium. Republic.* Translated by B. Jowett. Edited with introduction by Louise Ropes Loomis. New York: Walter J. Black, 1942.

*Sauvage, Micheline, in collaboration with Marie Sauvage. *Socrates and the Human Conscience.* Translated by Patrick Hepburne-Scott. New York: Harper, 1960.

Chapter 4

Duckett, Eleanor Shipley. *Alcuin, Friend of Charlemagne: His World and His Work.* New York: Macmillan, 1951.

Creighton, Mandell. "A Schoolmaster of the Renaissance: Vittorino da Feltre" in *Historical Essays and Reviews.* Edited by Louise Creighton. New York: Longmans, Green, 1911.

*Lamb, Harold. *Charlemagne: The Legend and the Man.* New York: Bantam, 1963.

*Quintilian. *Quintilian on Education.* Selected and translated, with an introduction by William M. Smail. (Classics in Education Series, No. 28). New York: Columbia University Teachers College.

*Woodward, William Harrison. *Vittorino da Feltre and Other Humanist Educators.* (Classics in Education Series, No. 18.) New York: Columbia University Teachers College, 1963.

Chapter 5

*Bainton, Roland H. *Here I Stand: A Life of Martin Luther.* New York: New American Library, 1963.

Richter, Friedrich. *Martin Luther and Ignatius of Loyola: Spokesmen for Two Worlds of Belief.* Translated by Leonard F. Zwinger. Westminster, Md.: Newman Press, 1960.

Von Matt, Leonard, and Hugo Rahner, S. J. *Saint Ignatius of Loyola.* Translated by John Murray, S. J. Chicago: Henry Regnery, 1956.

Spinka, Matthew. *John Amos Comenius, That Incomparable Moravian.* Chicago: University of Chicago Press, 1943.

Painter, F. V. N. "John Amos Comenius" in *Great Pedagogical Essays: Plato to Spencer.* New York: American Book, 1905.

Chapter 6

Pestalozzi, Johann Heinrich. *The Education of Man: Aphorisms.* Translated by Heinz and Ruth Norden, with introduction by William H. Kilpatrick. New York: Philosophical Library, 1951.

Silber, Kate. *Pestalozzi, the Man and His Work.* London: Routledge and Kegan Paul, 1960.

Chapter 7

Smith, Nora Archibald. "Friedrich Wilhelm August Froebel" in *Encyclopedia Americana,* Vol. XII, New York: Americana, 1950.

Chapter 8

Morgan, Joy Elmer. *Horace Mann: His Ideas and Ideals.* Washington, D.C.: National Home Library Foundation, 1936.

Tharp, Louise Hall. *Until Victory: Horace Mann and Mary Peabody.* Boston: Little, Brown, 1953.

Chapter 9

Gilchrist, Beth Bradford. *The Life of Mary Lyon.* Boston: Houghton Mifflin, 1910.

Goodsell, Willystine, editor. "Emma Willard, Educator and Builder," "Catharine Beecher, Pioneer of Education in the West," and "Mary Lyon, Pathfinder of College Education for Women" in *Pioneers of Women's Education in the United States.* New York: McGraw-Hill, 1931.

Harveson, Mae Elizabeth. *Catharine Esther Beecher, Pioneer Educator.* Lancaster, Pa.: Science Press Printing Co., 1932.

Lutz, Alma. *Emma Willard, Daughter of Democracy.* Boston: Houghton Mifflin, 1929.

Stowe, Lyman Beecher. *Saints, Sinners and Beechers.* Indianapolis: Bobbs-Merrill, 1934.

Chapter 10

Heffron, Ida Cassa. *Francis Wayland Parker: An Interpretive Biography.* Los Angeles: Ivan Deach, Jr., 1934.

Ketcham, Richard. "Faces From the Past" (article on Booker T. Washington), *American Heritage,* Vol. XIII, No. 6 (October 1962), p. 11.

Schilpp, Paul Arthur, editor. *The Philosophy of John Dewey*. New York: Tudor, 1951.

Spencer, Samuel R., Jr. *Booker T. Washington and the Negro's Place in American Life*. Edited by Oscar Handlin. Boston: Little, Brown, 1955.

*Washington, Booker T. *Up from Slavery: An Autobiography*. New York: Bantam, 1959.

General

*Curti, Merle. "Education and Social Reform: Horace Mann," "Henry Barnard," "The Education of Women," "The Black Man's Place: Booker T. Washington," "Francis Wayland Parker, Democrat," and "John Dewey" in *The Social Ideas of American Educators*. Paterson, N.J.: Littlefield, Adams, 1959.

*Frost, S. E., Jr. *Introduction to American Education*. Garden City, N.Y.: Doubleday, 1962.

*Reed, Edward, editor. *Peace on Earth: Pacem in Terris*. The Proceedings of an International Convocation on the Requirements of Peace. New York: Pocket Books, 1965.

SOURCES AND ACKNOWLEDGMENTS

In my search for authoritative and enlightening information on the nineteen timeless and timely teachers presented in this volume, I have gone to their own writings, their biographies, or translations of these, insofar as they were available; and I am especially indebted for valuable background material found in the publications listed here.

Chapters 1, 2, 3

Aristotle. *Collected Works.* Vol. IV: *Historia Animalium.* Translated by D'Arcy Wentworth Thompson. Edited by J. A. Smith and W. D. Ross. Oxford Press, 1910.

———. *Aristotle on Education.* Translated and edited by John Burnet. London: Cambridge University Press, 1903.

Diogenes Laertius. *The Lives and Opinions of the Eminent Philosophers.* Translated by C. D. Yonge. London: Bohn, 1853.

Grote, George. *Aristotle.* Edited by Alexander Bain and G. Croom Robertson. London: John Murray, 1883.
———. *Life, Teaching, and Death of Socrates.* Extracted by O. W. Wright from Grote's *History of Greece.* New York: Stanford & Delisser, 1859.

Hyslop, James Hervey. *The Ethics of the Greek Philosophers: Socrates, Plato, and Aristotle.* Edited by Charles M. Higgins. New York: Higgins, 1903.

Plato. *The Dialogues of Plato.* 4 vols. Translated by B. Jowett. 2 vols. Oxford: Clarendon Press, 1871.

Plutarch. *Plutarch's Lives,* Vol. IV. Edited by A. H. Clough. Said to be translated by Dryden. London: A. L. Burt, 188–.

Xenophon. *Memorabilia of Socrates.* Translated by J. S. Watson from the *Anabasis and Memorabilia of Socrates.* New York: Harper, 1860.

Chapter 4

Quintilian. *Quinctilian's Institutes of Eloquence or the Art of Speaking in Public.* Translated with an introduction by William Guthrie. London: Dutton, Richardson, Lea, 1805.

Sister of Notre Dame, A. *Vittorino da Feltre: A Prince of Teachers.* Edited by Dom Bede. New York: Benziger, 1908.

West, Andrew Fleming. *Alcuin and the Rise of the Christian Schools.* New York: Scribner's, 1892.

Chapter 5

Hughes, Thomas A. *Loyola and the Educational System of the Jesuits.* London: Heinemann, 1906.

Laurie, Simon S. *John Amos Comenius: Bishop of the Moravians.* London: Cambridge University Press, 1899.

Luther, Martin. *The Life of Martin Luther.* Compiled by M. Michelet. Translated by William Hazlitt. London: Bogue, 1846.

———. *The Table Talk of Martin Luther.* Translated and edited by William Hazlitt. London: Heinemann, 1906.

Monroe, Will S. *Comenius and the Beginnings of Educational Reform.* Edited by Nicholas Murray Butler. New York: Scribner's, 1900.

Chapter 6

Guimps, Roger de. *Pestalozzi — His Life and Work.* Introduction by the Rev. R. H. Quick. New York: Appleton, 1904.

Pestalozzi, Johann Heinrich. *Leonard and Gertrude.* Translated and abridged by Eva Channing. Boston: Heath, 1907.

Pinloche, Auguste. *Pestalozzi and the Foundation of the Modern Elementary School.* New York: Scribner's, 1901.

Chapter 7

Froebel, Friedrich Wilhelm August. *Autobiography of Friedrich Froebel.* Translated and annotated by

Emilie Michaelis and H. Keatley Moore. Syracuse: Bardeen, 1906.

Marenholtz-Bülow, Baroness Bertha M. von. *Reminiscences of Friedrich Froebel.* Translated by Mrs. Horace Mann. Boston: Lothrop, Lee and Shepard, 1877.

Snider, Denton J. *The Life of Friedrich Froebel, Founder of the Kindergarten.* Chicago: Sigma, 1900.

Chapter 8

Hinsdale, Burke A. *Horace Mann and the Common School Revival in the United States.* New York: Scribner's, 1900.

Mann, Mary Tyler. *Life and Works of Horace Mann.* 5 vols. Boston: Lee and Shepard, 1891.

Chapter 9

Beecher, Catharine E. *Educational Reminiscences and Suggestions.* New York: Ford, 1874.

Beecher, Lyman. *Autobiography and Correspondence.* Edited by Charles Beecher. 2 vols. New York: Harper, 1864.

Fairbanks, A. W., editor. *Emma Willard and Her Pupils or Fifty Years of Troy Female Seminary (1822–1872).* New York: privately printed by Mrs. Russell Sage, 1898.

Fisk, Fidelia. *Recollections of Mary Lyon.* Boston: American Tract Society, 1866.

Hitchcock, Edward, and others. *The Power of Christian Benevolence: Illustrated in the Life and Labors of Mary Lyon.* Northampton, Mass.: Hopkins, Bridgeman, 1851.

Lord, John. *The Life of Emma Willard.* New York: Appleton, 1873.

Gilchrist, Beth Bradford. *The Life of Mary Lyon.* Boston: Houghton Mifflin, 1910.

Chapter 10

Dewey, John. *Democracy and Education.* New York: Macmillan, 1916.

Giffin, William M. *School Days in the Fifties.* "Autobiographical Sketch of Francis Wayland Parker." Chicago: Flannagan, 1906.

Jenkins, Ralph C., and Gertrude Chandler Warner. *Henry Barnard: An Introduction.* Hartford: Connecticut State Teachers Association, 1906.

Steiner, Bernard C. *Life of Henry Barnard, the First United States Commissioner of Education.* Washington, D.C.: Government Printing Office, 1919.

Washington, Booker T. *Up from Slavery.* New York: A. L. Burt, 1901.

General

Cubberley, Ellwood P. *Readings in the History of Education.* Boston: Houghton Mifflin, 1920.

Marshall, Robert A. *The Story of Our Schools: A Short History of Public Education in the United States.* Washington, D.C.: National Council for Social Studies, 1962.

Ulich, Robert, editor. *Three Thousand Years of Educational Wisdom: Selections from Great Documents.* Cambridge, Mass.: Harvard University Press, 1963.

I want to express particular appreciation to my good friend Edith Patterson Meyer for her encouragement and helpful suggestions on this project.

I owe thanks also to numerous newspapers, television and radio programs, to *American Education*, and to the "News and Trends" sections of the *NEA Journal* for information gathered on Presidential messages, school statistics, and other public service reports.

I must thank the publishers of the following books: Ridge Press for permission to quote on pages 84–85 from *Pacem in Terris: Peace on Earth*, an encyclical letter of Pope John XXIII; Philosophical Library for permission to quote on pages 115, 125, 139–140 from Heinrich Pestalozzi, *The Education of Man; Aphorisms*, translated by Heinz and Ruth Norden; and Houghton Mifflin Company for permission to quote on page 136 from *Readings in the History of Education* by Ellwood Cubberly; and on pages 197, 231–240 *passim* from *The Life of Mary Lyon* by Beth Bradford Gilchrist.

I am indebted further to the editors of the *Saturday Review* for permission to use the excerpts quoted on page 57 from "The Need for Radical Reform" by Harold Taylor (November 20, 1965); on page 196 from "Rosemary Park: New President of Barnard" by Terry Ferrer (April 20, 1963); on page 251 from "The Genuine Educational Frontiers" by William Van Til (April 18, 1964); also, on page 251, from "The Realm of the Spirit" by Frederick Mayer (April 18, 1959).

I appreciate, too, the permission from the editor of the Metropolitan Art Museum *Bulletin* to adapt, on pages 42–43, from *"Aristotle Contemplating the Bust of Homer"* by Theodore Rousseau (January 1962) and from the editors of *Life* magazine for permission to quote on page 84 from "A Search for Something More Than a Com-

munity of Fear" by John K. Jessup, *Life*, March 5, 1966.
© Time Inc.

Finally, I am deeply grateful to General Omar N.
Bradley for taking time from his busy schedule to send
me a copy of his speech "A Decent Respect for Human
Intelligence," given at St. Albans Convocation, November 5, 1957; and for granting me permission to quote
from it on page 251.

Rose Friedman

INDEX

This book presents fifteen pioneer teachers who helped mold the underpaid and once scorned job of teaching into a respected profession.

Following Socrates, here are Plato and Aristotle; then three teachers of medieval Europe; and the great preacher-teachers, Martin Luther, Ignatius of Loyola, John Comenius. Today antipoverty programs have inherited the aims of eighteenth-century Heinrich Pestalozzi. Friedrich Froebel's insistance that no child is too young to learn is bearing fruit in moves to make nursery schools as well as kindergartens part of the public school system. Horace Mann more than anyone else was responsible for the acceptance of the public school idea itself.

Here are three women who worked to prove that women are as capable of being educated as men. Here in brief, finally, are Henry Barnard, first U. S. commissioner of education; Francis W. Parker of the University of Chicago; Booker T. Washington of Tuskegee; and John Dewey of Columbia.

Hopefully, getting to know these few among many great teachers will inspire young people to enter a profession in which opportunities are wide and rewards increasing.